The Revelation of Light

Exploring Our Psychic Worlds

OTHER BOOKS
by Robert R. Leichtman, M.D. & Carl Japikse

Active Meditation
Forces of the Zodiac
The Art of Living (5 volumes)
The Life of Spirit (5 volumes)
I Ching On Line (4 volumes)
Celebrating Life
Working with Angels
The Way To Health
Making Prayer Work
The Act of Meditation
Healing Emotional Wounds
The Role Death Plays in Life
The Light of Learning

by Robert R. Leichtman, M.D.
Fear No Evil
Recovering from Death and Other Disasters
Faith Fatigue
From Heaven To Earth (6 volumes)

by Carl Japikse
The Light Within Us
Exploring the Tarot
The Tarot Journal
Love Virtue

The Revelation of Light

Exploring Our Psychic Worlds

by Robert R. Leichtman, M.D.
& Carl Japikse

ARIEL PRESS
Atlanta – Columbus

No Royalties Are Paid on This Book

This book is made possible
by a gift to the Publications Fund of Light
by Judith R. Ross

THE REVELATION OF LIGHT

 Printed in the United States of America. Direct inquiries to: Ariel Press, 88 North Gate Station Drive #106, Marble Hill, GA 30148.

ISBN 0-89804-171-6

Table of Contents

To
All Members
of Light
Past, Present, and Future

Introduction

An Agent of Light

The path to enlightenment begins with an understanding—the understanding that we are a being of light. We possess, on loan, bodies of flesh, feeling, and thought, but these are only temporary residences. The real home of our selfhood is a body of light. Our bodies of flesh, feeling, and thought serve their function, and then they pass, but our true nature in light does not pass. Neither does it fail.

We are made as spirit; spirit is the cause of our being and all which happens to us. This spirit is a spark of divine energy; as it seeks expression as an individual, the spark glows and radiates, producing light. This is not physical light, which is feeble and dim, but the light of consciousness: immortal, unlimited, and creative. It is the substance of our humanity, the wellspring of our individuality, talent, wisdom, love, courage, and joy.

It is important to recognize this inner nature of light and distinguish it from the form and activity of the personality. Since we are a being of light, we ought to be inspired by this light, motivated by this light, and healed by this light. Yet often we are not.

The problem is one of becoming aware of our true identity. Through many eons, the light—which is our true self—has projected its radiance into the shadows of form, seeking to illumine that which is obscured. In the process, however, our personal sense of identity, which should be filled with light, has been blurred; we have identified with the shadows. We have come to think of ourself in terms of our experiences, perceptions, reactions, hurts, achievements, and associations—instead of as light. The poet Robert Frost captures this dilemma poignantly:

I have been one acquainted with the night.
I have walked out in rain—and back in rain.
I have outwalked the furthest city light.
I have looked down the saddest city lane.
I have passed by the watchman on his beat
And dropped my eyes, unwilling to explain.

To properly honor the light within us, we must look beyond the night. We must renew our acquaintance with light. Primarily, this means identifying with the soul and its plans, rather than the personality, with its wants, complaints, and difficulties.

An analogy which helps illustrate why this is important is the nature of physical light as it expresses itself through a light bulb. The bulb is the form through which the light shines, and yet it is not light. Nor can it produce light by itself. Only when it is connected to a source of electricity can the light bulb actually give off light.

Unless connected with spirit, our personality is no better able to produce the light it is designed to express than a light bulb that is not connected with electricity. Enlightenment is never produced in the personality alone; it is the result of integrating the daily life of the personality with the purposes and life of spirit.

It is this dynamic interplay which causes the light of our being to shine in the physical world.

Enlightenment has little to do with being able to see white light, "open the third eye," or run white light energy up and down the spine. Instead, the enlightened individual is one who is focused in the light of the soul and is able to sustain that focus through his daily self-expression. The hallmarks of enlightenment are mastery of the emotions, the ability to comprehend the "mysteries" of life, and the capacity to work creatively in life.

It should be obvious, therefore, that the single most important step toward enlightenment is the effort to make the personality a more fit vehicle for the light of God. Enlightenment is the product primarily of the effort to express our talent, wisdom, love, courage, and joy as fully as possible in our daily activities. Or, to put this idea a little more poetically, enlightenment is achieved by learning to breathe in and breathe out the light of the soul. We breathe in the light by attuning ourself to the ideals of life and filling our awareness, our appreciation, and our adoration with these ideals. We breathe out the light by seeking to invest these same ideals in all that we do—in our work, relationships, hobbies, and recreation.

In all these endeavors, our goal must be to unite the events and needs of the personality with the actual light of the soul. This involves four basic stages:

1. Discovering the light. It may be tempting to dismiss this stage of enlightenment as trivial, but it is not. Long after the personality intellectually and emotionally recognizes that there is a soul and its nature is light, it still insists on substituting something less than real in lieu of light. In confronting a difficult relationship, for example, the personality may go through the motions of consulting the soul as to how to proceed—and then block out the light and do what it prefers anyway. And yet the self-deception is accepted; the personality contentedly believes it is fulfilling the desires of the soul, even while gratifying its own wishes and whims.

To *discover* the light, therefore, we must begin by distinguishing between light and shadow. Light impels us to grow. It leads us into paths of rightness. It causes us to increase our skills, our understanding, and our compassion. It is found in our highest aspirations, ideals, values, and maturity—never in our wishes and good feelings.

2. Comprehending the light. Once the light is discovered, it must be understood and rightly interpreted. This stage is not an easy one to master, as light is multidimensional by nature. It cannot be understood only in three-dimensional terms; the study of light forces us to think in terms of immortality and infinity as well. It forces us to give up one limitation of thought after another.

Understanding the nature of our personal destiny is a good example of this difficulty. It frequently occurs that certain events befall us that make little sense in the context of our work, needs, or other activities. The personality is often confused by these events, and may even question the wisdom of a soul which could let them happen. It may doubt the benevolence of the light itself. Such doubts and puzzlements, however, are simply signs of incomprehension. The vastness of light has escaped our narrow view. Inevitably, such circumstances do fit a larger pattern of continuity, either helping us learn a lesson we have been studiously ignoring for a long time, or preparing us for opportunities as yet unseen in the shadows of daily life—but perfectly obvious in the light of spirit.

Another instance of the difficulty of comprehending the light is in the difference between the conventional expressions of the ideals of love, joy, beauty, and wisdom and their actual realities in light. All too often, for example, the expression of love is marred by sentimentality, possessiveness, and jealousy. Enlightened love, however, has nothing to do with these distortions.

Thus, to *comprehend* light, we must seek always to look for the higher perspective which makes sense of our feelings, attitudes, challenges, and conflicts. When light is properly comprehended, it removes all doubt, second-guessing, and confusion.

3. Integrating the light. At the level of the soul, we are a being of light, but the personality remains in shadow. The third stage of enlightenment, consequently, is the integration of the light of the soul with the needs and activities of the personality, so that our daily self-expression radiates light as well. In practical terms, this means blending the light of our love, joy, courage, and wisdom into the unredeemed or imperfect elements of our attitudes, habits, values, talents, and activities.

As the path to enlightenment is trod, the crabby, blighted, mean, and ignorant areas of our personality slowly ebb away, and are replaced by light. We treat others better than before. We view ourself with more dignity; we act with a greater measure of gracefulness. We eliminate our tendencies toward carelessness, dishonesty, and laziness. In this way, we become a more effective person, by ridding ourself of that which does not embody the light.

This is not a matter of accommodation, where we layer a thin icing of niceness over an otherwise hostile and selfish personality. As Jesus put it, "No one can serve two masters." It is not possible to serve the light and the shadow both; therefore, to *integrate* the light into the personality, we must remove all traces of shadow. We must purge that which is impure and welcome into our consciousness that which will honor the light. We must harmonize the personality with the plans and purposes of the soul.

4. Expressing the light. Again Jesus said, "Men do not light a lamp and put it under a bushel, but on a stand, so it gives light to all in the house. Let your light so shine before all men, that they may see your good works and give glory to your Father who is in heaven." The work of enlightenment is a private undertaking between the personality and the soul, but the fruits of enlightenment must be shared with all. Light is radiant; it is against its nature to be contained and held private. If we are not working to express light in all we do and think and say, we are not really dealing with light at all—just a glimmer.

We *express* the light by building, serving, and healing with it. Light seeks to create; as we become creative, even in humble ways, we express the light. Light seeks to serve; as we contribute to its service, we express the light. Light seeks to heal; as we focus its healing warmth, for the benefit of others, ourself, and civilization, we express the light.

Usually this creativity, serving, and healing is far from spectacular. It is carried out quietly, without fanfare, in the context of our work, relationships, interests, and social responsibilities. By striving to enlighten life and leave it a little better than we found it, we express light.

These four stages of the process of enlightenment

apply not just to individuals, of course, but to the groups and institutions of humanity as well. Churches, governments, science, and civilization need enlightenment as well as individuals. So do education, literature, business, the arts, and other significant avenues of human endeavor. The same principles apply. Little is gained just by polishing up the shadowed forms of these institutions or enterprises, through the infusion of large amounts of money or worry. What is required is a genuine perception of the lighted ideal within these endeavors, a comprehension of how it can best be honored, hard work in harmonizing the group involved with the direction of light, and continued effort to express the highest measure of light possible.

If we persevere, the reward is great. We become an agent of light.

The lessons in the *Enlightenment* series all deal with this theme—becoming an agent of light. The intent is to demonstrate what it means to discover the light, comprehend it, integrate that light into the life of the personality, and express it in all we think, do, and say.

In their original form, the lessons of light were grouped in seven categories. Each lesson covered a topic from one specific category. This book, *The Revelation of Light*, is a compilation of the fourteen lessons from *Enlightenment* that deal with the topic of psychic skills and awareness. The other six categories present other lessons that are also important to the development of the agent of light. These six categories are:

- The nature of archetypal forces and symbols and

how they express light through religion, mythology, literature, music, and the events of individual life.

- Self-expression and why it is important, with lessons on the male/female principles, creativity, healing, the enlightened work ethic, and group expressions.
- Integration—of soul and personality, the mind and emotions, values and self-expression, and the individual with groups.
- Enriching the mind—through reading, appreciation of the arts, interaction with the fourth and fifth dimensions, observation of life, and interpretation of dreams.
- The process of learning, and its importance to the life of spirit.
- Interacting with other kingdoms of life and discerning the value of their relationship with humanity, thereby expanding our awareness of the full scope of divine life.

Enlightenment is a call to action, not just fodder for further intellectual study. Becoming an agent of light is an active process, requiring the direct involvement of the individual seeking enlightenment. We must understand that all elements of life are suitable targets for the work of enlightenment; only as we individualize the light does it radiate through our own life.

We do not need to become a missionary in Africa to find light—or retire to a monastery or ashram and ape the movements of saints. Our work, hobbies, relationships, responsibilities, and efforts to grow are the suitable and proper vehicles for light. They provide us rich opportunity for discovering the light, comprehending it, integrating it, and expressing it. Unless we focus the light through these activities, whatever they may be, we will not really be doing its work.

There is no moment too insignificant to use this formula. After all, if we cannot be an agent of light in the midst of annoyance or pettiness or simple fatigue, it is hardly reasonable to expect to be an agent of light in more spectacular circumstances. If we cannot be faithful in a little, it is foolish to believe we could be faithful over much. If we cannot heal, build, and serve with light, even in the smallest of ways, we cannot rightly expect to be healed, strengthened, or served by the light ourself. Therefore, to receive light, we must learn to contribute light. To be enlightened, we must become an agent of light.

Which prepares us for becoming the light itself.

1.

An Introduction To the Psychic Worlds

Not too many centuries ago, the world was thought to be flat. Christopher Columbus believed otherwise and proved, by sailing to the Americas, that the planet is actually a globe. This discovery was a great step. Unfortunately, it has not been pursued to its fullest implications. We are still too "flat" in our thinking about the world we inhabit.

The earth is not just a physical object, orbiting about a physical sun. It is a complete system of spiritual expression, an appropriate vehicle for the One in Whom we live and move and have our being. As such, it is really three worlds in one.

The first world is the physical world. Of the three, this is the most familiar to us, for we can see and touch and hear and taste many of its phenomena. But even at this level, there is much that our flat perceptions these three worlds comprise a complete system for spiritual self-expression: the earth. They also make up the environment in which we live. But the two psychic worlds—the worlds of the emotions and the mind—remain largely unknown and unexplored to the vast majority of us.

There are several reasons why this is so. The most prevalent is simple ignorance: many people have never heard of the psychic worlds and are therefore unconcerned with them. They do not realize that they live in an incomplete reality. Others do know about the psychic worlds, but believe it to be evil or sinful to explore them. This is a wholly irrational belief, but nonetheless common among superstitious people. In addition, there is the attitude among certain spiritual aspirants that any exploration of the psychic worlds would be a distraction from the "real" work of reunification with the divine; these people scoff at anyone who professes an interest in the psychic worlds, assuming them to be their inferiors.

Yet all of this is nonsense; the psychic worlds are part of the environment in which we live and move and have our being, and are therefore part of the fabric of God's expression. To believe that it is evil or sinful to explore the psychic realms of life is to believe that God Himself is evil and sinful. To believe that it is unspiritual to develop psychic talents and skills is to enshrine ignorance. It simply makes sense to learn about the psychic worlds.

After all, there is more to life than just God and

miss—for example, the energy fields and activities which have recently been captured by Kirlian photography.

The second world is the world of the emotions, or the astral world, as it is sometimes known. This is a more subtle dimension of life than the physical world, made of qualities and forces rather than forms. We live in this world, for we have emotional perceptions and reactions, but we are not alone here, any more than we are alone in the physical world. There are many kinds of life at this level, and many types of expression. The phenomena of this world cannot be perceived physically, however; they must be perceived psychically.

The third world is the world of the mind, the most rarefied of the three. Like the physical world, it is a world of forms, but these are thoughtforms—ideas, concepts, plans, theories, and convictions. We live in this world, too, for we have thoughts and ideas, but we are no more alone here than we are in the other two. There are many kinds of life in the mental world, as well as a wide spectrum of expression. As in the astral world, however, the phenomena of the mental world cannot be perceived physically; they must be perceived psychically.

These are not three separate worlds, but one. They interpenetrate one another, occupying the same space, although in different dimensions. They also interact with one another. An event in the emotional world is apt to trigger events in the physical and mental worlds; a thought at the mental level is likely to provoke responses emotionally and physically. Together, all of the higher astral and mental levels. Their silly pronouncements and charades clearly advertise that they have no more ability to see or hear with understanding than the densest materialist. With them, we need not be concerned.

But for the sincere explorer of life, the agent of light, developing an awareness and understanding of the psychic worlds is an important part of cultivating the eyes that see, the ears which hear. And this is a blessing, as Jesus clearly stated; it is a significant attribute in the work of enlightenment.

It is as though each one of us carries with us our own compact "wisdom laboratory." No one can manufacture wisdom for us; we must do it for ourselves. But to make our wisdom laboratory functional, we must conduct experiments with it—making observations, testing conclusions, and exploring new regions. This brings us into the realm of the emotional and mental worlds.

The kinds of experiments we can conduct in the psychic worlds are beyond number. They can be experiments in healing, in which we invoke a variety of different inner sources and evaluate which ones respond most effectively—and to what kind of invocation. Or they can be tests of the divine energies which are tapped by various kinds of prayer, and to what end.

Amid the "beakers" and "retorts" of our wisdom laboratory, we can actually observe the impact of different emotional expressions—the emotional impact of others on us, and our impact on them. In the psychic worlds, for example, it is possible to see that anger really the physical plane. There are many points in between—levels of awareness which are, in many ways, closer to God than the physical world. By becoming acquainted with these psychic levels, we learn a great deal about human nature, the creative process, consciousness, and the principles of life. We acquire a larger perspective toward life and become more holistic in our outlook. We enrich our understanding, knowledge, and talents.

It is time to set aside the old prejudices of "flatness" and recognize the full, multidimensional scope of life. We do not live in the physical plane alone, but in a world which is both tangible and psychic. We therefore ought to become more familiar with the psychic realms in which we dwell.

Jesus often concluded His parables and comments with the phrase, "He who has ears, let him hear" or "He who has eyes, let him see." To anyone with a good psychic awareness of the mental plane, it is clear that this phrase was His subtle way of suggesting that these stories or statements, as figurative as they might seem, have an actual reality at one of the psychic levels. And yet, they will be incomprehensible to a person who lacks trained psychic perception.

This is not to suggest that anyone who professes to be psychic has a full understanding of the psychic worlds. There are many ignorant people who play at the game of pretending to be psychic; there are others who possess some small capacity to operate in the lower realms of the astral world, yet have no perception at values, that also would represent a psychic perception.

By becoming more knowledgeable of the psychic worlds, many important secrets of life become known to us. But even more significantly, it leads us to a very important revelation.

We discover the existence of light.

The goal of working in the psychic worlds should always be the revelation of light. Light does not originate in either the emotional or the mental sphere; it radiates from the heaven worlds, which are even higher levels of consciousness. And there are plenty of areas on both the emotional and mental levels where light is obscured, just as it is in the physical world. Astrally, light is obscured by selfishness, excessive fantasy, anger, hostility, jealousy, and pettiness. Mentally, light is obstructed by prejudice, illusion, narrowmindedness, and criticism. Nevertheless, the psychic worlds reveal the presence and glory of light far more than the physical plane. To become a genuine agent of light, we must therefore become aware of the psychic worlds, their life, their phenomena, and their divine function.

In doing so, we increase our awareness in a number of ways, all of which can become building blocks for a greater level of spirituality.

• We become more aware of our subconscious, which exists almost entirely in the psychic worlds. As a result, we learn to discriminate between fantasy and reality, between the personal and the universal, and between dark and light. We learn the basis for intelligent self-discipline.

is destructive and damaging to the physical nervous system. We can also observe the patterns of pollution and distortion in mass consciousness and directly perceive the ways trends and fads develop and are spread.

Not all experiments in the psychic worlds would involve the negative, however. Many artists experiment extensively in their wisdom laboratories with the right expression of beauty, color, and light. They are definitely aided by psychic perceptions, even if they do not label them as such. A parent who is aware of the psychic components of a child's character will know with certainty what opportunities to set before the child, what strengths to encourage, and what lessons to emphasize.

Indeed, the psychic worlds hold many secrets for us. They can be ours—but only if we develop the "eyes to see." This does not mean we must become clairvoyant or clairaudient; it basically means that we must become aware of the psychic worlds, strive to account for them in whatever we do, and interact with them with common sense.

If we learn something about how our subconscious works, for example, by monitoring our stream of associations and evaluating our habit patterns, that amounts to a psychic perception. If we study the creative process and learn to invoke a higher quality of inspiration for the work we do, this would be a psychic perception, too. If we develop a more profound rapport with another person, to the point where we are truly able to understand his attitudes, feelings, and most heartfelt birth—what has retarded us and what has benefited us. These psychic forces are even more important than physical conditions, yet are generally ignored by the average person. This is perhaps a blessing, for the average person would have a hard time managing much psychic input; but for the agent of light, awareness of these sources of influence is a great asset.

This increased awareness in no way has to be personal or subjective, although many people suppose that it would be, since our perceptions of the psychic worlds occur in our own wisdom laboratory. It is true that as long as the laboratory is turned toward personal preoccupations, worries, and problems, our perceptions of the psychic worlds will be highly subjective in nature. But so will our perceptions of the physical world.

Once we discipline our thoughts and feelings so that we can enter our laboratory and work without the discoloration of preference and prejudice, however, we discover that the psychic worlds are objective. Even the fantasy of the "Peter Pan Department" of the astral world is objective, meaning that it exists independently of our own imagination. When observed by different psychics, all will report basically the same phenomena.

The reason why the psychic worlds seem subjective to so many people is that they are approached improperly, like a myopic child trying to read a book upside down. We insist on giving our dreams intensely personal meanings; we labor hard to give images and symbols which arise in meditations a personal significance. The key to handling the phenomena of the psychic worlds

• We become more aware of the full environment in which we live and move and have our being. It is in the psychic worlds that the influence of zodiacal forces becomes obvious—and how to use them creatively. It is in the psychic worlds that the subtle influence of mass thought and feeling on personal attitudes is revealed. It is in the psychic worlds that the real seeds of disease and disorder can be observed. It is in the psychic worlds that the growth of character and quality in form can be evaluated.

• We become more aware of the true bonds of human relationships, which have a literal existence in the psychic worlds. We are thus able to observe both the positive and negative aspects of human interaction—the destructive impact of psychological manipulation on the one hand and the nurturing power of goodwill and compassion on the other.

• We become more aware of the multidimensional nature of form—that every physical object has an emotional and mental counterpart. As a result, we learn a great deal about the continuity of life.

• We become more aware of the operation of universal principles and divine laws, by observing them in a more complete context. Many of the phenomena of the physical plane have no real meaning in a physical context alone; their significance becomes clear only when corresponding events in the astral and mental worlds are recognized, too.

• We become more aware of the psychic forces and conditions which have influenced our growth since not at all necessary to be psychic in the conventional sense of the word. Much can be discovered simply by monitoring the attitudes, thoughts, and insights which arise in our perceptions as we consider a certain "seed-question" over a period of time. Here is a seed question which can be examined profitably during the coming eight weeks:

"How do my attitudes and thoughts change as I go from place to place in my daily activities: from home to work, to shopping center, to church, to theater, to restaurants, and so on?"

For example, if we are in a good mood at home, happy and cheerful, but then become grumpy and sour while shopping at the grocery store, what does this suggest about the emotional climate of that particular store? If this change happens just once, it may be a fluke of the moment, but if it repeats itself frequently, what can we deduce about the psychic impacts we are experiencing?

Or, if we are attending a lecture in which the speaker is describing the nature of the spiritual life, and we gradually start feeling more and more irritable and angry, what is the meaning of these perceptions? It could be that dark elements within us are not responding well to this person's message—but it may also be that the psychic message this speaker is projecting toward us is very much different than the lovely words he is uttering aloud.

Emotional perceptions are the easiest to make, but it is also important to evaluate the impact of the psychic objectively, however, lies in viewing them as impersonally as possible.

In addition, it ought to be understood that the phenomena of the astral world are fourth-dimensional in nature, and the phenomena of the mental world are fifth-dimensional. This means they are far more complex and many-faceted than physical phenomena, which are restricted to three dimensions. It is therefore quite possible that two skilled psychics could view the same object or condition astrally or mentally and describe it in very much different ways—and yet it is still the same object.

After all, if two people were asked to describe a mutual friend physically, they would probably be in near agreement. But if asked to describe their friend's emotions, habits, self-image, and innermost thoughts, the descriptions might well be radically different, because each has observed different facets of their friend. And yet the person is the same in each case—and very definitely objective.

If this fundamental objectivity of the psychic worlds is kept in mind, there is no reason for any intelligent person to refrain from exploring them. Indeed, to choose not to utterly ruins our ability to be objective in life, for we are ignoring large and significant portions of life.

When we fail to recognize the psychic worlds, for whatever reason, we obscure the revelation of light.

To exercise our awareness of the psychic worlds, it is

worlds on our thoughts. Is there one particular place, for example, where we are able to think more clearly and creatively than others? Why is that the case? What psychic elements interfere with good thinking in certain locations, and which factors promote it elsewhere?

By evaluating this seed question in these and many other ways, it will be possible to construct a great deal of practical knowledge about the psychic worlds of our life—all without being overtly psychic!

We will touch a new awareness of light, and become far more profoundly aware of major aspects of the body of the One in Whom we live and move and have our being.

These are the revelations of the psychic worlds.

2.

The Dangers of Psychic Perception

To the average person, the human being is a life form of flesh and blood, living and acting on a globe of rock and dirt. But as the average person is transformed into a spiritual aspirant, a different perspective emerges. The aspirant learns to look beyond the flesh and blood of form and the limitations of materialism; he discovers that our inner thoughts, motives, values, and beliefs determine who we are far more than our appearance or physical heritage. Eventually, he comes to realize that our true nature—and the true nature of all life—is light, the light of the divine life within us.

How is it that one person can perceive the light within, while so many others cannot? The answer is a simple one. As the spiritual aspirant embarks on his journey of self-discovery, he slowly (perhaps unconsciously) develops psychic skills and intuitive abilities. He learns to register the presence of life at nonphysical dimensions—emotionally, mentally, and even spiritually. He discovers the relationship of life at all these levels, and eventually comes to understand that these levels are actually just one great stage of life. It is our capacity for discernment which is fragmented and must be developed level by level, until we are able to perceive the light within the form at all levels.

When we use our physical eyes to read the print in a book, it is a process we call "seeing." When we use our psychic or intuitive senses to read the character of another person, it should likewise be considered part of the process of seeing, only at more subtle levels. Unfortunately, society has not yet come to accept the subtle perceptions of clairvoyance, clairaudience, and clairsentience as extensions of our ordinary senses. But they are.

And they are most useful. It is only by cultivating our psychic abilities that we can directly explore the emotional and mental worlds around us. It is only by developing intuitive skills that we can explore the realms of spirit which are the heart of our life. It is only by learning to see and hear subtly that we eventually reveal the light within us.

The mastery of psychic perception is relatively rare, but even an emerging ability to explore the inner realms of life is of great value, and something every aspirant should cultivate. Through psychic investigations, we can study human consciousness, its development, its problems, and ways to help it overcome its typical problems. When found in a trained psychologist, for instance, the capacity to diagnose emotional problems psychically makes the ordinary tools of psychological diagnosis look crude and primitive in comparison.

Nevertheless, as useful as a well-trained ability to behold life psychically is, the spiritual aspirant must understand that there are dangers along the road to psychic development. We are handicapped in our efforts to develop psychic skills, because these are skills we must develop internally, within our own mind and imagination. Somehow, we must learn to deal with the presence of *ourself*—our attitudes, prejudices, fears, and convictions, all of which can easily distort the accuracy of our psychic perceptions.

If we proceed with common sense, there is not much danger of self-deception. But there is a facet to psychic perception which sometimes undermines our common sense. It can be exciting and thrilling to experiment psychically, almost like being part of an effort to solve a deep mystery. These very factors can cause us to suspend our common sense, and fall into the pit of self-deception. Indeed, this failing is so common among the average spiritual aspirant that the first step in developing psychic skills and abilities must always be to learn to recognize the dangers of psychic perception and how to neutralize them.

In examining the dangers of psychic perception, we must adopt the perspective of consciousness, not the personality. The ultimate function of psychic skills is to help us expand our awareness in useful ways—to embrace the inner dimensions as well as the physical. If we try to judge dangers from a purely physical perspective, we will surely err.

With this assumption in mind, the risks and problems posed by the development of psychic skills fall into five basic categories:

From within ourself. Our own beliefs, ignorance, and expectations can color or block out all or part of a legitimate psychic signal. As an example, let us assume that we believe that all blond people are weak in character and dishonest. If we are psychically focused on someone who happens to be blond, we will probably conclude that he or she is weak and dishonest—without even knowing why we have drawn this conclusion. Just so, if we believe that all fear stems from the way we were treated by our father as a child, then we will believe that everyone we encounter who has problems with fear spent a traumatic childhood.

From limited perception. There is a tendency among psychics to stop with first impressions, without plumbing the depths of a subject thoroughly. A psychic may be able to tell that you are not in harmony with your spouse, but if he stops there, this "insight" may cause great injury. It may lead you to believe that the only solution is a divorce. And yet, if the psychic probed a little further, it might well be revealed that in spite of this outer disharmony, there is a strong link at inner levels which transcends it and can be invoked to solve the problems causing the dissension, reestablishing a solid relationship.

From social traditions and mass consciousness. For centuries, we have corrupted society's understanding of life with terrible misconceptions and superstitions. The very existence of strong fundamentalist beliefs about sin and the devil, for example, serves to color our psychic perceptions, even if we do not accept the concept.

From the inherent plasticity of the psychic planes. The first level we encounter as we seek to expand our awareness is the emotional. These levels of consciousness are highly plastic in nature and tend to mirror whatever we happen to think and feel—or want to think and feel. The substance of this level is very easily molded by our own projected thought. And so, if we carry with us a belief that all people are sinful, we will project that silly notion onto anyone we might study psychically, thereby distorting our perception of him. We may even create an artificial image of the other person astrally and study it, rather than the real person.

From the inherent pollution of the psychic planes. The lower psychic worlds are the levels where the mental and emotional bodies of the human personality have their actual existence. As a result, the psychic planes have become a dumping ground for the emotional and mental waste products of the human race. Since the average human is not very saintly, the content of these emotional and mental outpourings is rather polluted. Centuries of malice, selfishness, prejudice, fear, ignorance, and superstition have served to contaminate these planes to the point where these thoughtforms often obscure the truth of what exists and transpires in the psychic worlds. It is for this reason, for instance, that so many psychics predict major catastrophes and earth changes. These predictions are shaped by mankind's basic belief that we deserve to be punished—not by the actual divine plan for the planet and the race.

The reason for itemizing these dangers of psychic perception is not to scare off anyone—or give fuel to those who believe that psychic work is evil and should be avoided. It must be remembered always that psychic exploration is the only way in which the light within us is discovered and revealed to the rest of the world. It is therefore important to proceed with the development of our psychic skills—but with common sense and caution, knowing the dangers that lie ahead.

Fortunately, there are sensible steps we can take to minimize these dangers. None of these sources of danger is actually that difficult to manage, so long as we keep in mind that all psychic perception occurs within our own awareness. *It is our own naïveté and gullibility which invoke and invite deception and inaccuracy.* If we arm ourself with intelligence and foresight, we can eliminate almost all of the risk.

There are five major precautions we must make:

1. We must stand guard against wrong motives. Many people cultivate psychic skills to satisfy a thirst

for the fascinating, bizarre, and flattering. They very quickly find themselves speaking with "ancient masters," "walk-ins," and people from other planets. Most of what is said is banal double-talk and metaphysical platitudes, but these people are not interested in substance—only excitement and sensation.

The more proper motive for psychic exploration is an intense desire to learn more about ourself, our problems and how to solve them, and the invisible worlds we live in. If this is indeed our motive, then we will have an innate capacity to sense the light within genuine revelations and communications and dismiss that which is devoid of light.

It must be understood that if we pursue psychic growth with the wrong motive, we may be taking a short road to disaster. Flattery and platitudes may seem harmless enough, but in the long run they can be quite damaging. Real problems need real solutions. Fooling around with fantasy tends to distract us from getting down to the practical work of solving our problems and making a practical contribution to life. It also tends to remove us from the rich sources of opportunity, healing, and satisfaction in life.

2. We must stand guard against excessive emotionalism and reactiveness. Any strong sentiment or reactive tendency can color accurate psychic perception. Fear is the worst of all, both at conscious and subconscious levels. As we harbor a fear, it automatically attracts from the astral plane the very conditions we fear. Fears stimulate our imagination to "see" the worst

possible thing happening to us. Obviously, if we try to explore our psychic worlds while laden with fears, this automatic process will seriously interfere with accurate perception.

Other emotions and sentiments can create the same kind of obstacles. Pessimism, resentment, and self-pity all need to be cleaned out of our character before we can expect to see clearly in the psychic worlds. A pessimistic attitude will bias the psychic toward predicting disaster, setback, and failure. Anger will seep into the observations of a psychic and subtly saturate them with paranoia and hostility. Even what the psychic wishes for himself or herself may subtly affect perceptions of the inner life, because the wish life is one of the strongest and least understood phenomena of human awareness.

It is therefore important to set an emotional tone of cheerfulness, helpfulness, and optimism as we start our explorations of the psychic worlds.

3. We must stand guard against egotism. Some people are so self-absorbed and stuffed with so much self-importance that they set themselves up for considerable self-deception. Egotism tends to send out a "psychic call" that will draw to it whatever will support its arrogance and unfounded confidence, while simultaneously blocking out anything of a contradictory nature. As a result, psychics who are ruled by their ego run a grave danger of succumbing to input which makes them look important, while overlooking and ignoring legitimate insights which point out the best way to learn what we need to know. They need a short course in inspired humility.

4. We need to stand guard against ignorance. The ability to perceive the psychic worlds does not in any way make a person wise. It is quite possible to be a stupid psychic, and this is worse than not being psychic at all. A stupid psychic is one who *ipso facto* assumes that any strong and spontaneous feeling or impression must be a psychic revelation. This is a very dangerous assumption. All input that we receive about life, whether psychic or intellectual, needs to be weighed in the scales of a discerning mind. As we receive insights, we need to ask ourself: Does this help me answer my questions or solve my problems? Can I make practical use of these ideas? Have I been given ideas which help me understand my life and the direction I am heading—or have I just been flattered and conned?

5. We must guard against an overheated imagination. Some folks habitually take three dots and assume it is a map to lost treasure. These people hear that a "George" wishes to speak to them and immediately assume it to be George Washington! Such people are almost always excessively fascinated with information about past lives, soul mates, and the like. But they ignore more practical information—insights into how they can be a better spouse, a more responsible worker, or a more supportive parent. They need to devote themselves to learning to discern the truth behind outer appearances, and dedicate themselves always to responding only to the truth.

There is no quick fix or magic formula in eliminating

the dangers of psychic development. Our protection lies primarily in the basic attitude with which we approach our investigations, and the measure of reliability and stability we have demonstrated in the past. If we have shown a weakness towards shallowness and phoniness, it will be much harder to protect ourself from these dangers than if we have always been as honest and as helpful as possible. Given this healthy attitude, however, there are a number of steps we can take:

1. We need to rededicate ourself to the highest understanding and level of wisdom we can contact. This dedication will tend to cut through the fluff and nonsense of our overheated imagination and any secret desire we may have for psychic thrills and chills. By dedicating ourself to truth and clear perception, we do two things: we alert the subconscious to knock off the nonsense, and we invoke our higher self to protect and guide us in our studies.

2. We need to cultivate a genuine humility toward our higher self and the truth. We need to set aside the silly idea that all truth is relative and admit that there are forces, powers, and intelligences greater than ourself. We need to pay attention to these forces and learn what we can from them, instead of trying to boss them around and make them serve us. True humility sets us on a wavelength of receptivity to the higher self.

3. We need to practice detachment and dispassion. If we are at all emotionally involved in the outcome of our researches—hoping for one particular result over another—we will automatically create whatever it is we

want to see or hear. The only solution is to learn to work impersonally, keeping our personal preferences, worries, and fears from intruding.

4. We need to rely on our common sense. The life of the inner planes is not fundamentally different than life in the physical, just more subtle. The more bizarre, fanciful, or exotic our impressions or insights become, the more likely it is that we are deceiving ourself. The insights we receive should be common sense solutions to our daily problems.

5. We need to be pragmatic. In other words, we need to look at the "bottom line" of whatever information we receive psychically. Can it be applied productively in daily life? Can it be verified? Does this input help us understand life better? If it does, then accept it. But if there is no practical application to the ideas we receive—if they are just more platitudes and truisms, we should be skeptical of them.

It is not necessary to be involved in a program of psychic development to cultivate the basic attitude that will protect us against psychic deception. In fact, it is probably easiest to learn this attitude in nonpsychic circumstances—in the ordinary circumstances of daily life.

Our work begins as we select an ordinary aspect of life. This could be the way we take advice from friends, listen to the news on television, interpret personal suffering, or respond to authority.

Our object is to discern how we respond to and interpret these ordinary circumstances of life. In listening to friends, for example, do we listen to what they are saying—or do we listen to what we think they are saying? How quickly do we decide what their point is?

Are we interested in the truth of what our friend says—or just our own opinion? What is our motive? Do we interact with humility? Do we have a secret agenda? Are we listening with common sense? Do we look for a pragmatic application to what we hear?

It is important to let this lesson take us beyond the obvious levels of appearance. We must look beyond the surface of statements and search for their real meaning. We must likewise evaluate the meaning of our responses. Do we react to the evening news with fear and a sense of personal revulsion? Then how could we examine the psychic side of life objectively?

The best way to train ourself to perceive life psychically is to begin by learning to perceive physical life without distorting it.

3.

Our Psychic Mechanism

There is no doubt that interest in psychic phenomena is rapidly growing. Two out of every three adults accept the possibility of psychic perception. At the same time, however, there seems to be little indication of any corresponding growth in understanding how psychic perception occurs. Most stories in the popular media simply dismiss any need to understand by stating: "No one yet knows." Many psychics also feed this misconception, largely because it adds an aura of mystery around them.

This is intellectual laziness. The psychic process can be understood and, like any skill or habit, learned through proper training. In fact, the operation of psychic perception is much more commonplace than the average psychic or journalist would have us believe.

Just as we all have a fundamental capacity to learn to speak and write English, ride a bicycle, or any of a thousand ordinary skills, all of us also have the basic mechanism we need to become psychic. Few of us have spent any time training this mechanism to operate on command, but this does not diminish its existence or capacity to function.

What is this mechanism? Why has science not discovered it?

Actually, science *has* discovered it; it is one of the most well-known facets of human psychology. The human being consists of three levels of awareness: the conscious personality, the subconscious, and the unconscious. The conscious personality is that small part of us that we use to focus on moment to moment thought, feeling, and action. The subconscious is the underlying structure of our memories, dreams, convictions, beliefs, feelings, and habits which is the true force of personality. It can be tapped and known by the conscious person as needed. The unconscious is that part of our awareness beyond the control of the conscious person; it may include repressed feelings and unwanted memories on the one hand, or the patterns and plans of our higher self on the other.

The conscious person is not normally psychic, but the subconscious is. This does not mean that psychic impressions *originate* in the subconscious; if they did, they would be no more significant than any wish or fantasy. The impressions we receive psychically come from others, from our environment, and perhaps even from our higher self. But they are perceived and registered in the subconscious, where they take their place among the memories, prejudices, and preferences stored there.

Learning to become psychic, therefore, consists largely of learning to register these impressions as they arrive in the subconscious and transmit them to our conscious awareness in a timely fashion. This simple explanation may disappoint those who want to keep as much magic and mystery in psychic phenomena as possible, but it is true nonetheless.

Of course, some psychics and mediums will flatly disagree with this assessment. They will claim that they receive their impressions directly from God or some other higher intelligence. But they are confusing the source of the message with their own mechanism for perceiving it. Even when we listen to a friend or colleague in physical life, we are still registering these impressions in the subconscious. It is not the eyes that see nor the ears that hear. These are merely the senses that register the vibrations of the world around us. We see and hear only once the vibrations have been transmitted to the subconscious, interpreted, and relayed on to our conscious awareness.

In the same way, if we behold an angel psychically, we do not hear or see this being directly. Our impressions are registered first in the subconscious, interpreted (which may include screening and censoring), then relayed to our conscious awareness–if our conscious awareness is receptive to such input.

To develop psychic ability, therefore, we do not need to train some mystical "third eye" or learn to work with exotic energies. We do not need to entertain strange beings. Primarily, we must understand the role of the subconscious in the psychic process and train our own awareness to register and transmit psychic impressions into our conscious perception.

The importance of the subconscious to the psychic process becomes obvious when we realize how easily the contents of the subconscious color or condition what we see of the world around us—and how we interpret what happens to us. A cheerful, happy child, for instance, will tend to view the events of life as a game to be played or something that will entertain it. An overworked, harassed executive, on the other hand, will set a sober mental tone that filters out everything except that which is immediately relevant to the work at hand. A bigot will militantly screen out all evidence except that which supports his or her favorite prejudices.

The same processes influence psychic perceptions. *Every psychic impression which is registered by the subconscious is perceived, interpreted, and directed by a subconscious that has already been conditioned by the force of our beliefs, memories, values, and moods.* If we do not believe in psychic perception, for example, this belief may be so strong that our subconscious will simply deny that the psychic impressions we do receive mean anything, and will never direct them to our conscious attention!

In much the same way, if a kind and gentle person were to send loving, healing thoughts to a hostile, paranoid individual, the subconscious of the latter would register the strength of the kind gesture but totally distort the quality of it. The paranoid's innate defensiveness cannot conceive of anyone wanting to help him, and therefore assumes that he is being manipulated or used in some way.

The ability of the subconscious to distort input in this way may seem fantastic at first, but it is just the normal operation of what is known as the "associative mechanism." The associative mechanism is the process the subconscious uses to relate our current experiences and perceptions to our memories and our reactions to them. It is this mechanism that lets us encounter new experiences and make sense of them. Without it, virtually every experience would seem totally new—and incomprehensible.

When we meet someone for the first time, our associative mechanism immediately evaluates him. It takes all kinds of clues—the tone of his voice, the physical appearance, the subjects discussed, even the sound of the name—and compares them to our extensive subconscious records of other people we have known. From this comparison, it makes instant deductions, and we form a "first impression"—often quite erroneously. Perhaps this person reminds us of a schoolmate who betrayed us. We will immediately be suspicious, and probably have no idea why.

The same process works with psychic inputs. We

may be walking through a shopping mall and suddenly see someone who reminds us of a family member. At second glance, we decide that the resemblance is more imaginary than real, and shrug it off. But a real message has been conveyed to us. Our subconscious has become aware of an important psychic message from our relative, and has cast around for something in the physical plane to remind us of this person. The trained psychic will sense the association being made and perceive the message. The average person, however, will miss it entirely.

It should be obvious, therefore, that our ability to perceive anything accurately—be it physically or psychically—depends upon the content of our subconscious and the health of our associative mechanism. If our wish life is strong and relatively uncontrolled, it will color and distort everything we perceive with our fantasies, desires, and prejudices.

If we are angry or jealous, for example, these reactive patterns will tend to skew everything to justify our hostility and paranoia. To develop a useful measure of psychic perception, therefore, we must know how to begin—by disciplining and restructuring the subconscious so that our perceptions match reality, not our perversions of it. We must become aware of our beliefs, prejudices, fears, and doubts, so we can discount them as they appear in our predictions and impressions. Even more importantly, we must establish a *baseline of thought and feeling* which gradually reflects the ideal ways we want to respond to life—as opposed to our default reactions of anger, jealousy, selfishness, and pride.

Until this baseline is established and operational, we will never know what is a legitimate psychic insight—or just our own immaturity. If we are sitting in a theater and are suddenly overwhelmed with fear, is it our own—or is it the fear of the person sitting next to us? The average person will never know. But the person who has established a baseline of thought and feeling free of fear instantly knows this is a psychic impression, and responds accordingly.

Eventually, as we work to train the associative mechanism and create a coherent baseline, we discover that the content of the subconscious actually serves as well as a kind of antenna for psychic signals. If we are hostile, we will be much more attuned to threats, insults, and the darker side of human nature than a person of goodwill. If we worry excessively, we will be much more attuned to the possibility of loss than another person would be. On the other hand, if we have trained ourself to respond to creative inspiration, we will be able to tap innovative ideas more quickly than others. If we have trained ourself to work with healing energies, we will be able to turn them on and off almost at will.

Being psychic has nothing to do with being one of God's chosen people. It is a skill that can be learned by all of us. The key is learning to understand the role the subconscious plays—and train it to behave in helpful, productive ways.

The first step in training the subconscious must always be to clean up the bulk of negativity we have allowed to accumulate there. The fact that we carry negativity around with us does not make us a bad or evil person; all of us build up a residue of frustration, worry, fear, resentment, and guilt as we make our way through life. But these residues are distinctly unhealthy, especially when they distort the way we view life. To develop psychically, we must learn to control them, subdue them, and eventually remove them. Otherwise, the reactiveness of our anger, fear, envy, bitterness, and grief will seriously distort incoming psychic signals.

This does not mean that we must become a saint in order to work psychically. It simply means that we must take effective steps toward reducing the burden of negativity we carry with us. It also means exercising extra caution when entertaining psychic impressions about certain "hot" subjects.

A strong rejection of reincarnation, for instance, may block out all contrary evidence that tries to come through. A psychic with such strong disbeliefs may be amazingly accurate in all areas but that one, yet consistently distort his impressions about reincarnation. Just so, a lack of knowledge of medicine may block out helpful information that might heal others. A prejudice against Christianity might block out the psychic impressions which would clarify the meaning of some passage of Scripture.

As we clean up the subconscious of our personal

residues, however, we will find that it is not the fault of the subconscious that these distortions occur. It is just the way in which we are using it. Indeed, the subconscious is actually designed to support and facilitate the process of psychic perception, not limit it. And this will occur if we take the simple step of cultivating a healthy belief system which respects and trusts in our higher intelligence and power. In this way, we can attune the subconscious to the higher elements of life and create in it the expectation that valuable insights will be coming to us psychically. Naturally, this respect and trust for our higher intelligence must be sincere and heartfelt.

A second important step in training the subconscious to cooperate with the psychic process is to cultivate a measure of detachment. If we are too involved personally in the outcome of our psychic work, our subconscious will be more interested in pleasing us than in delivering accurate information. We must therefore cultivate a capacity to view life impersonally, as though our personal reactions did not matter. Until the subconscious actually believes this there will be a constant potential for distortion.

The subconscious has its actual existence on the psychic planes. Contrary to traditional beliefs, it is not just a bunch of electrochemical reactions in our brain; the subconscious is made of psychic matter from the astral and mental planes. It does not die when the body dies; it continues to live on as the real substance of our personality. The average person finds this hard to understand, because the part of the subconscious we are familiar with is the earthbound part—the part that is focused in daily experiences in the physical plane. But like a camera lens, the subconscious can actually be focused in many directions.

Part of training the subconscious is to learn to focus it inward, so that it is more responsive to psychic signals. Then psychic perception becomes a controlled process, not a random one. Indeed, the more we develop psychic awareness, the more protected we are against spurious psychic impressions. It is not uncommon for an average person to walk into an office poisoned by tension and competitiveness and suddenly get a headache. Psychologists blame this on "free floating moods." It is actually a psychic registration of the environment.

A well trained psychic would probably not be affected in this way. Instead, he would register the presence of pollution in the office, but not interact with it to the point of getting a headache. His subconscious discipline protects him.

Indeed, the best form of protection in working psychically is our own sense of individuality. Our knowledge of who we are and what we stand for creates a definite boundary between our subconscious and the psychic planes in which we live and have our being. This explains why small children are often naturally psychic—their sense of individuality is not yet fully developed. It also explains why neurotics are so often troubled by fears and worries; their "psychic skin" is dangerously thin. They need to strengthen their concept of selfhood.

This does not mean we should become a thick-skinned bigot. Such a person is protected from psychic intrusion—but at the cost of being almost totally blind to psychic impressions. The gentle and humble person who nonetheless has a strong sense of selfhood is, by contrast, ideally prepared to work psychically. There is enough flexibility to respond to psychic signals, yet enough strength to ignore harmful or misleading input.

It is for this reason that the ancients always began psychic instruction with the adage: "Know thyself and to thine own self be true." If we know who we are, can work impersonally, and treat the truth always with respect, we will find little difficulty in mastering the skills of psychic perception. Above all, however, we must view psychic work not as an intellectual exercise but as an expression of our vital humanity. Our subconscious is, in many ways, the "womb" of the creative as well as the psychic processes. As such, it can respond to psychic and intuitive signals in one of three ways:

1. It can abort them.
2. It can distort them and produce a monster.
3. It can nurture them and help them become a part of our own self-expression.

The subconscious is a magnificent part of our humanity. We need to respect it and work to improve it, rather than polluting it with bigotry, falsehoods, deception, and prejudice. We must teach it to become aware of all of life, so that it can lead us on our journey toward the revelation of the light within us.

The key to training the subconscious to act wisely with psychic input is to become aware of and seize control of our reactiveness.

In the evening, in a reflective state, we should focus on our strongest reaction, positive or negative, of the day. What events and perceptions followed this reaction? How much were they colored by our reaction? Were we able to regain control? How long did it take?

After a week or two, we need also to start looking for strong inner moods and states of mind that significantly color our outlook and actions. Where do these inner moods come from? Are they part of our accepted baseline of thought or feeling? Or were they an intrusion? Did we control them?

The same kind of review must also be made of our memories and associations. As strong feelings and moods arise, to what past events do we associate them? Do these moods remind us of the past—or is it in fact the unresolved problems of the past that are reawakening these moods? What can be done to regain control of this process?

As we answer these questions, we will be exploring first hand the nature of our own associative mechanism. To the degree that we cleanse it and reactivate it with the courage and confidence to work with psychic impressions, we will be taking a major step toward becoming psychic.

4.

Exploring Our Astral Environment

The first inner world we begin to explore as we work to develop psychic skills consciously is the astral plane—the world of the emotions. In fact, even though the term "psychic" embraces both the astral and mental planes, most uses of "psychic" nonetheless refer to the astral plane. Indeed, the vast majority of psychics operate exclusively at the astral level.

This astral world is nothing less than the emotional body of the planet earth. We are linked to it through our own body of feelings—our astral or emotional body. In actual fact, our connection to the astral plane is much more than a mere linkage. We are immersed in it. Every human being on earth lives within this environment and is heavily affected by it.

Indeed, the astral plane is the primary environment in which most people live and act. Ten to fifteen percent of the world's population is focused primarily on the physical plane; a similar percentage is beginning to operate primarily on the mental plane. But the remaining seventy to eighty percent of the human race is polarized on the astral level. They react to life instead of thinking about it; their self-expression is filled with opinion, emotion, and feeling, rather than rational thought. They tend to make decisions, choose goals, and shape attitudes based on their emotional experiences and reactions.

Because the majority of people throughout the world is emotionally focused, the strongest influences in mass consciousness are opinions and attitudes, instead of ideas and principles. Our values may be enunciated by thoughtful people, but they are interpreted and promulgated emotionally. As a result, even if we happen to be mentally polarized, we are still surrounded by a primarily emotional environment every moment and day of our life.

The astral world, in other words, is an intimate, important part of our life—even if we are trying to leave our own emotional focus behind. And yet, as important as it is to all of us, very few people know much about it. It has not been studied much by psychologists; it has not been charted extensively by explorers of the mind. What little we do know is widely considered to be superstition or speculation.

This is most unfortunate, because the astral plane is the first level of awareness we "step" into as we strive to move from the dense physical plane to the more spiritual levels of life. It is not a level of spirit, any more than the physical is, but it must be thoroughly explored and penetrated through in order to reach, eventually, the mental world and the worlds of spirit beyond.

It is therefore with the astral plane that we must begin our excursion into the psychic worlds.

It is not necessary to be able to "astral travel" in order to explore this psychic dimension. In fact, it is often a detriment; most of the people who claim to be able to travel astrally never accomplish anything signficant! They end up exploring the astral world much like a tourist would go sightseeing—seeking out sensationalism instead of insight, appearances instead of awareness. They become little more than astral clairvoyeurs.

In fact, we do not even need to be in a trance! One of the major forces comprising the astral world is the human subconscious—which includes our own subconscious. So, we can profitably begin exploring the nature of the astral world by examining carefully our own life—in specific, the quality, force, and movement of our feelings, attitudes, and memories.

Let's assume that we are in a foul mood. A series of highly unpleasant events has just unfolded in our life, and it all seems overwhelming—as though it would be impossible to reassert dominion over our life. Seeking relief from this mood, we take a stroll outdoors. As we walk along, the beauty and harmony of the natural sights all around us begin to reawaken responsive chords in our own subconscious. Soon, the more mature elements within our subconscious have become strong enough that they are able to restrain the foul negativity, and we regain balance. We may even feel grateful, both for the beauty and harmony in nature and for the beauty and harmony within our own attitudes and feelings.

Obviously, something more powerful than just the physical expression of beauty and harmony through nature is at work here. We have exposed the grimness and negativity of our bitter mood to direct contact with astral forces of beauty, harmony, and peace. They are refreshing our subconscious, just as a bath or shower cleanses and refreshes the physical body after a sweaty, grimy day. This should not be too surprising. The flowers, trees, and animals of nature have astral bodies. So does the sun and the atmosphere. Plants and trees in particular are often majestic exponents of refined astral forces such as strength, harmony, and patience. In addition, a walk through nature's realm may well bring us into contact—unconsciously—with nature sprites, invisible humans, and angelic powers that can likewise purify and uplift us emotionally.

The intermingling of these refined astral forces with our own feelings, cleansing and purifying the negative ones and strengthening the positive ones, happens beyond our conscious awareness—until we begin to make the effort to expose ourself to it, be drawn into its reality, and study our reactions to it.

This example illustrates a powerful point. Moving throughout the astral plane is not the same as taking a jet to Detroit. Astral movement occurs by association, rather than in a linear direction. We travel astrally, in other words, every time we review the emotional content of a memory or brood about the future.

Let's assume that we are plagued periodically by the memory of a missed opportunity—perhaps the failure to tell a parent how much we appreciated and loved him before he died. As we revisit the memory months or years later, we "travel" again to the sadness or guilt that we first experienced—plus we energize this pattern with yet another layer of guilt or sadness. In this way, we carry our painful memories with us, making them stronger and more powerful each time we brood on them.

As this example suggests, the seemingly innocuous activity of brooding on worries and fears is not as harmless as it may seem. It deepens the negative mood and solidifies the thoughtform of this feeling in our memory. It also magnetically attracts potentially overwhelming flows of similar astral energy from relatives, friends, associates, and mass consciousness. It is as though we are being inundated by floods of negativity from every direction—and we are.

Ideally, our interaction with the astral world should be enriching, uplifting—like a walk through nature. Our investigation should fill us with the reflected light of God, not the darkness of human pessimism and fear. The astral world can be a constant source of cheerfulness, peace, harmony, strength, affection, and enthusiasm—if we teach ourself to tune into the higher astral dimension of religious services, the loving aura of a mother encouraging a child, the joy of a true celebration, and so on.

At present, however, it is not always easy to locate these sources of astral blessing. Large portions of the astral world that we must interact with have been strongly polluted by our very human contact with them. They have been clouded with fear, worry, pessimism, grief, greed, and suffering—the sum of human negativity over the last several centuries. As a result, an unguarded, fleeting moment of casual sadness can at times unleash huge inpourings of negativity and despair.

One of the classic examples of this problem in our modern society is the damage that has been done by certain angry protest groups. Even when these groups have legitimate complaints and valid solutions, the anger and fear they embrace through their loud protests does far more harm to the astral world than the injustices they are protesting at the physical level! Good-hearted people are often inclined to support their protestations—until we actually examine the foul stench they have generated astrally. When we realize the darkness in which some of these groups operate—and the total absence of any contact with divine forces or spiritual realities—the agent of light is forced to re-evaluate their worth and mission.

In the individual, repeated expressions of anger or fear accumulate and form habitual patterns that govern behavior. In mass consciousness, the same kind of pollution occurs. As individuals and groups of people behave petulantly, angrily, or fearfully, they add their personal rubbish to an ever growing pile of human emotional garbage. This willful pollution of the astral world is then accepted as "normal," and we thoughtlessly continue to act in violent, fearful, or brooding ways—as groups, businesses, and nations, not just individuals.

Moreover, we encourage and endorse this pollution. Each time a psychologist encourages a group of patients to explore their anger, the pollution of the astral world grows worse. Each time the nightly news spreads fear and gloom through rumor, the contamination of the emotional world deepens.

The saddest part of all is that most humans almost never explore any part of the astral world except these garbage dumps. As a consequence, they cheat themselves immeasurably.

Every emotion or feeling we express opens a doorway to the astral world. If we are being patient, kind, or optimistic, the inflowing astral force will be enriching and healthy. But if we are being crabby, hateful, or bitter, the incoming emotional wave will overpower, confuse, and deplete us. Whether positive or negative, our present emotional state magnetically links us with the same emotional force at the global level.

When we thrill to the beauty of flowers in the spring, in other words, we are "plugging into" the full force of beauty as expressed by humanity since the beginning of time. It is as though we had hooked up with a world wide web—but of the emotions, rather than computers. The simple act of beholding azaleas in bloom can therefore become a psychic experience enabling us to explore the real power of beauty at the astral level.

But when we read salacious accounts of horrible events in a newspaper and reenact these events in our own imagination, we are likewise plugging into a world wide web—a network of lust, gossip, and cheap thrills that is the sum of human tawdriness since society first conceived of tragedy.

These are regions of the astral world that no sane person would willingly choose to explore. And yet all of us do—every time we succumb to negative emotions such as anger, crabbiness, fear, hate, or grief. Moreover, the longer we let our personal attention dwell on any of these destructive emotions, the more intense our contact with its global counterpart will be. We will run a serious risk of over-energizing our own emotions with astral force that is not our own—and cannot control.

This is the reason why seemingly normal people may become unduly depressed for several weeks, with no apparent reason. They have allowed a moment of sadness or grief to plug them into the world wide web of depression—and they have found themselves to be almost powerless to free themselves.

No human being is exempt from this process, although the agent of light learns to control it, by a) dwelling in the light of the astral world, not its darkness and b) working to transform elements of emotional negativity within himself, so that he is less susceptible to constant exposure to the global web. In general, all of us need to understand—

- We energize our own emotional moods and attitudes. Our feelings are not dictated to us by the acts of others and the events of life. We choose whether our reaction to these conditions will be noble and uplifting or spiteful and harmful.

- We magnetically feed our personal moods and attitudes with similar negative forces drawn in from the astral world. This process occurs automatically, at subconscious and unconscious levels, depending upon the prevailing qualities in our own subconscious.

- We regularly distort our perceptions and judgments about life, based on the patterns of wish and opinion found in the subconscious. An angry protestor, for example, tends to find evidence that supports his hateful agenda all around him, even though there is far greater evidence which does not. The quality of his astral focus simply discards all of the evidence that does not agree with his position and highlights the evidence that seems to support it. He may even believe that he is doing God's work—even though the presence of anger and hostility immediately disqualifies him.

- We continuously project our own emotional mood, attitudes, and opinions onto others—and the whole of the astral plane—to the point of feeding and provoking similar responses in others. It should be understood, in this regard, that it is not necessary to verbalize a mood or attitude in order to project it. A religious leader might well be talking about the need to love one another while psychically projecting his or her scorn and disdain onto the assembled crowd.

Such psychic interactions with the astral world are

neither rare or unusual; even the most earthbound person "invokes" the realities of the astral plane every day. Together, mass consciousness wades through the muck and murk of the polluted astral world—and then wonders why there are wars, drug addiction, and terrorism.

It is up to the agent of light to take responsibility for cleaning up the pollution—first, in his own life, and second in the life of humanity. No one ever needs to be bogged down or overwhelmed by fear, grief, or anger. The astral world is meant to inspire and motivate us with cheerfulness, courage, and compassion.

And it will—but only if we learn to call upon these divine forces and direct them into our own life.

There is only one safe way to explore the astral world—and just one safe way to conquer it. We investigate it by discovering our own emotions. We conquer it by learning to control our own negative emotions. As the ancients advised: "know thyself."

It is naïve to assume that just because our innermost feelings are invisible and seemingly silent, they are either neutral or harmless. It is equally foolish to believe that such emotions have no enduring influence on us or others, nor have a direct influence on our own perceptions and judgments about life.

Indeed, we have an obligation—if we ever want to become a proficient explorer of the psychic realms—to keep our focus in life positive, enriching, and healthful.

It would be silly to "explore" our anger so that we could be more in touch with global anger. Global anger destroys lives. Instead, we must seize the opportunity of an angry moment to cleanse and purge such feelings, replacing them with compassion. We must also learn how to reject the undesirable without becoming angry.

It would be stupid to "investigate" our fear so that we could be more in harmony with universal fear. Instead, we must eliminate fear from our own subconscious and learn to be more detached and constructive in our attitudes. We must also learn to cope with threats in a mature way.

It would be outrageous to "pursue" our personal bitterness about some injustice into the astral world. On the contrary, we need to purge bitterness from our memories and learn to accept the experiences life has brought us, not complain about them. We need to promote peace and joyfulness and justice without personal vengeance in world thinking.

We all live and move and have our being within this astral world. Only the weak, undeveloped person accepts his or her feelings as they are, saying: "I am what I feel." The agent of light sees his or her feelings as a doorway of realization.

The angry person can become compassionate.

The fearful person can become courageous.

The distrustful person can become faithful.

The irritable person can become peaceful.

The work of transforming our emotions is not a choice. It is an obligation. It is a duty.

It is an obligation to humanity.

It is a duty to our higher self and to God.

It is the only way to develop reliable psychic skills.

The work of transforming our emotions begins by selecting an ideal attitude we seek to acquire:

Cheerfulness.

Gratitude.

Affection.

Charitableness.

Serenity.

Confidence.

The first step is to reflect on two or three memories when we best expressed this quality. As we dwell on these memories, we must let our own expressiveness link us to larger forces of this quality globally. We need to dwell on all the many wonderful things going on in our life—and in life in general—that justifies this attitude. These memories and greater awareness become a seed for cultivating the ideal attitude.

As we reflect in these ways, we should anticipate times during the coming week when we will have the opportunity to express this wonderful quality. We must project the proper attitude onto our own future—to expected events and interactions with others. Then, we need to maintain this attitude as a steady state of feeling as best we can during the week.

As we work in this way, we gradually learn to focus our emotions. Instead of using them reactively, harshly, they become a force of constructive influence in our life.

We will also learn how to harness the psychic realities of the astral plan.

5.

Exploring Our Mental Environment

Once we have become familiar with the astral plane, the next inner world we need to explore, in order to develop psychically, is the mental plane—the realm of thinking. This mental world is more subtle and refined than the astral, yet operates under similar laws and principles. To some, in fact, it may seem sterile and uninteresting at first—in comparison to the drama and intensity of the astral plane. But this kind of perception is only the result of our faulty values and lack of refinement, not the reality of the mind.

The mental plane is a dynamic dimension where huge thought currents are constantly generating creative inspiration, guidance, and awareness. From the divine point of view, the mental plane is an outpost of the mind of God, an "out-picturing" of the divine plan. It is structured around the Big Ideas of divine design and operates with almost mathematical precision.

From our point of view, the mental plane is like a vast library of thought, filled with ideas, patterns, blueprints, and meaning. As we develop our own mind and thinking skills, we are meant to learn to interact with the mental plane and its powerful ideas. We are invited, by our higher self, to reach out mentally and explore this world in its furthest recesses, thereby enriching our own thinking abilities. At the same time, we are impelled by very human needs to make sense of life, acquire new skills, and discover better answers as we cope with our earthly struggles.

The mental plane is a great place to think. It is not nearly as contaminated by dark human feelings as the astral plane. There are some serious problems with pessimism, but nothing that compares to the astral problems of anger, hatred, despair, and envy. The mental plane is much closer, in terms of purity and refinement, to the spiritual forces of the divine mind. As a result, it is far easier to generate a powerful contemplative state while focused in the mind than in the emotions. Moreover, even the untrained mind is free of much of the astral tendency to personalize and color all perception.

In point of fact, thinking is what happens naturally on the mental plane—it is the *activity* of this level of existence. Culturally, we tend to believe that thinking occurs in the human brain, but this is not the case. Thinking occurs as the mind interacts with the forces of the mental plane. As elements of these thoughts are registered in the brain, we become conscious of them. Thoughts that are not recorded in the brain remain unknown to us. Nonetheless, they may influence us, even though we are unconscious of them.

If the mind is not well developed, its capacity to interact with the mental plane will be limited. It will likewise be erratic in communicating with the brain. Thinking will be an accidental occurence. But if the mind is highly trained, the situation is reversed. Communication with the brain becomes continual and rapid. At the same time, the capacity to inspect the wealth of knowledge of the mental plane expands. The mind becomes an intrepid explorer, able to inspect and examine the accumulated thinking of mankind, the blueprints and designs underlying all of creation, the trends and objectives of the divine plan, and much more. The mind is also able to exchange ideas mentally with other thinking entities.

In truth, the whole spectrum of thinking can be inspected and learned from, as we become skilled and comfortable in investigating the many wonders of the mind. The mental plane is nothing less than the dimension where human and superhuman thinking occurs—and interacts.

To understand the realm of the mind, we must take care not to define it too much in human terms, as though it were a giant invisible brain or computer in which we are somehow trapped. The essence of the individual mind is an emanation from the divine mind. As such, it is based on divine purposes and principles, and is organized along divine archetypal themes: order, justice, peace, goodwill, joy, beauty, harmony, and strength.

This is not to suggest that the whole contents of the mental plane are divine or pure. Good and powerful ideas can be distorted and diluted. But in spite of the thought garbage we may occasionally encounter, the mental plane is carefully organized along currents of divine thought.

The great philosophers of the human race have recognized this principle. Plato, for instance, held that all worthwhile thinking stems from a central Idea, and that this central Idea (archetype) is defined by God. Anything that begins to distort or dilute this central Idea confuses the thinking process, instead of enriching it. Such personalization and bias should be avoided, lest thinking be sabotaged.

Ideally, our schools and colleges should be organized in the same way, teaching the comprehension of one great central Idea. The degree to which modern education fails to fulfill this challenge illustrates the alarming lack of true thinking in our society today. Young people flock to universities today in unprecedented numbers in order to learn to think. But instead of having their minds and thinking skills attuned to a central Idea or archetypal thought, they are brainwashed by a strident, one-dimensional intellectual climate that colors—even poisons—their thinking, values, and priorities. They are being taught to respond only to the carefully-defined ideology of their professors—not to the full power of the archetypal mental plane. As a result, they end up interacting with only a tiny sliver of the mental plane—a carefully defined mental environment selected by their instructors.

These students do not learn to explore the mental

plane! They do not learn to turn on the light of the mind to cast out doubt, confusion, and distortion! They learn only to admire and respond to a highly restrictive congeries of convoluted ideas that traps them in pessimism and paranoia. Even this can be powerful enough to charge up great enthusiasm among students being exposed to ideas for the first time—but falls far, far short of what thinking can be. Even worse, it often entraps these students in illusions—the Big Lie—for a long time.

As agents of light, we need to comprehend that what we do not understand can indeed hurt us. What we do not know, or do not want to know, about the modern methods of learning and thinking can powerfully cripple both ourselves and society. For this reason, it is a spiritual duty to learn what the mental plane is and how to use its resources properly. This mental environment is alive, well, and a constant influence in our lives. It is clearly within our best interest to learn how to interact with it wisely.

After all, every one of our thoughts and ideas exists and takes shape within the mental plane! We are naturally responsive to whatever ideas come and go in our personal mental field—our own mind. To be a wise person, we need to know where the content of our thinking originates. Is it coming from the mind of God, as a Big Idea? Or does it derive from the sleazy doctrines of a radical politician—or the evening news on the television? It may just be a hangover from the thinking of an earlier generation—as in the resurgence of Fascist ideas in Germany today. Is it thinking—or is it Memorex®?

This interaction with the mental plane is reciprocal. At the same time that our own thinking is being subtly influenced by outside forces—our mental environment—we are likewise imposing our values and convictions on the mental world around us. If we latch onto an especially silly or destructive concept, we may well lead a number of others in addition to ourselves into confusion and false understanding.

In fact, the reactiveness of shallow thinkers is often the target of demagogues and militant religious leaders. The demagogue seeks to impose his (and now her) ideas on the thinking of others. This is a clear distortion of the ideal—that each of us should build our own mental structure of values and principles on what we know of the divine design. Demagogues, in short, put themselves squarely in opposition to God even if they invoke the holy name in every other sentence.

The same principles apply to the thought processes of whole groups. Our individual mind exists not only within the reservoir of human and divine thinking, but also within the smaller circumference of the cultural, national, and racial groups to which we belong. The values, traditions, and principles of these groups have a dynamic impact on our personal thinking—at least until we learn to transcend it.

The great danger of this kind of group influence is not that it will affect us, but that narrowly-focused factions within our group will subtly alter a key value or principle held by the group—with almost no one realizing that it is occurring. When the United States was founded, for example, self-sufficiency was a virtue to which everyone in our culture aspired. It is still paid lip service, but over the last 75 years, it has become only the shell of an ideal. The people of America have traded in self-sufficiency for security. As a result, we have in effect bartered freedom for paternalism and sold out democracy for a tyranny of special interests. This revolting turn of events has occurred without a single shot or a single vote; it was jerry-rigged by unscrupulous people at the level of the public mind.

Indeed, the only way to understand what is happening in our physical world is to see it in the context of the forces—divine and malign—that are being shaped at the mental level, and who is doing the shaping. It does not do any good, after all, to train ourself to think—and then align with the unspired but persuasive thought-forms of low-grade thinkers. We need to connect with the origins of thought—the divine design.

Even today, with our modern educational advantages, only a few people have taught themselves to interact consciously with the mental plane. Most people, even college graduates, remain mired in an astral focus. They may occasionally extend their awareness into the mental world, but on the whole they spend their time *feeling*, not thinking:

- Resenting their problems.
- Regretting missed opportunities.
- Fearing the competition—or colleagues.

This is what they observe other "thinking people" do, so they do it, too. They preserve the long-standing tradition of stewing in their dark emotions.

The real problem is that they do not even know that they are not thinking! As a result, their "thinking" becomes sloppy—they do not question the validity of thoughts and beliefs. They accept "spin" as though it were the truth, instead of propaganda. In lieu of listening, they distort, filter, and distill ideas until they conform with just what they wanted to hear—and believe.

Some people, of course, actively disdain the thinking process. They believe that emotions are more real and honest than thoughts, which they regard as artificial. They treat concepts as nothing more than products of their imagination. As a result, values, commitments, and principles are all *things* they have created at whim—and feel free to change at their pleasure. These are usually people who have no experience whatever in exploring the mental world. There is also a sizeable portion of the population who is afraid of genuine thinking, because they dare not confront the horrible truth about themselves.

Let it be clearly understood: access to the mental plane can be achieved in one and only one way. We must teach ourselves to think—and having learned, put our thinking skills to practice.

In order to understand this crucial point, however, we must first realize that most people do not think—even when they think they think! How is this possible? Quite simply, instead of probing into the mental plane and finding an idea that helps them solve whatever problem they are dwelling on, they reach only into the astral plane, where they snatch up whatever opinion, pseudo-fact, or popular trend reinforces what they already want to believe. They appear to think, but the process is occurring only superficially. They fail to comprehend the real issues involved, or develop any sensible plan for action.

Thinking is the process of investigating, understanding, and using ideas. All good ideas are based on archetypal realities—key Ideas in the mind of God. The goal of good thinking is always to penetrate as far as necessary onto the mental plane to tap and capture some facet of this archetypal presence. Shallow thinking, which scratches only the astral plane, leads to nowhere but increased confusion. Genuine thinking, by contrast, leads always to clarity, revelation, and creativity. That which was confusing becomes comprehensible.

In reflecting on our relationship with a colleague at work, for example, we might realize that certain habits this person expresses annoy us to a degree. The shallow thinker would dwell on the astral elements of these habits, and actually increase his or her annoyance. The profound thinker, by contrast, would look beyond the annoyance and focus instead on the mental values of cooperation, tolerance, and goodwill. It would become clear that the value of cooperating with others and respecting their talents far outweighs occasional feelings of irritability.

It is through this kind of exploration of mental archetypes that we teach ourself to think.

In order to explore the mental plane, therefore, we must first learn how to think. The most important element of such a quest is *curiosity.* This is because the substance of the mental plane actually responds to inquiry and study. All of the answers to all of the questions we could possibly ask already exist, in one form or another, at the mental plane. But in order to access these answers, we have to learn how to shape a question that will draw forth the proper answer.

The starting point of any mental inquiry, therefore, is to define *what we need to know*, whether we are asking for personal insight, a scientific or creative inspiration, or general understanding of human nature. We are not trying to snoop on life or gain secret knowledge; we are humbly and patiently researching what we need to discover.

A proper respect for the power of the mental plane is helpful. We must not forget that this is an extension of the divine mind; we have come to explore, not to loot and pillage. We are not rebelling against divine law; we are trying to understand it. We are not criticizing the way life has treated us; we are striving to comprehend it. We are not trying to prove that God exists; we are just trying to understand the forces at work in our problems and shape a desirable solution.

We have come to gather insight, not just speculate.

Our inquiry needs to be solution-oriented. We must invoke the best way of responding to the situation at hand, based on archetypal realities and patterns—not just something that will satisfy our wish life. The goal of thinking is not to feel good, but to know good! Once we have comprehended what the good is, we need to do good.

As we focus on our true goal—more patience, renewed optimism, or greater affection—we can then translate the force of the archetypal idea into a "seed thought." A "seed thought" is just what it sounds like—a few words which signify to us the embryo of a new, more enlightened way of acting. "Clear understanding," for example, might be an excellent seed thought to work on early in the process of learning to think. "God down here" might be a good seed thought for someone trying to practice the immanence of God.

A seed thought works by planting it in our subconscious, nurturing it so that it grows into a strong influence on our awareness and character. Repeated contemplation of a seed thought is an excellent way to incorporate divine force into our own self-expression.Always keep in mind that there may be a difference between the archetypal meaning of justice and our own personal views—or society's definition, for that matter. When many people use the word "justice," they mean vengeance, pure and simple. Yet there is no trace of vengeance in divine justice.

For this reason, we must make sure that our seed thoughts are filled with light, before we plant them in our fertile subconscious. These should also be impersonal, since they link us with archetypes. If we are just feeding our own desire for revenge, we would be better off not using our wounded version of justice.

We must therefore explore the divine presence within the seed—the germ of the archetype. We need to let the archetype itself expand our perspective on the issue at hand and all of life. It is this enrichment of our mind that lets us leave behind our personal wish life, so that we may gain access to the mental plane.

We can then frame our inquiry more intelligently:

If my thinking were filled with divine justice, how would this affect my values? My goals? My priorities?

How would it alter my emotions?

How would it change my behavior?

What would it impel me to do?

What would it impel me to stop doing?

Our goal is nothing less than to penetrate to the core of this archetypal thought. Only then can we tap the impelling force of this Big Idea—the power we need to act as an agent of justice in our life.

A simple exercise for learning to think archetypally is to choose an appropriate seed thought to examine and strengthen. This seed thought would represent a spiritual quality or archetype such as justice, harmony, order, beauty, peace, compassion, joy, or strength.

A short "catechism" can help us frame our investigation:

What is the nature of this seed thought as it exists archetypally and applies to the issues of life? What are its larger implications? Can we invoke the impelling power of this seed thought to produce change in our life? How can we apply the wisdom of our understanding to other issues of life? Can we use the power of the seed thought to heal problems at a cultural, ethnic, or national level? Can we use the seed thought as a springboard for understanding the mythic element and application of this archetypal quality?

These lessons will help us learn to think clearly at every relevant level of the mental plane.

6.

The Inner Dimensions of Forms

As we explore the astral and mental worlds psychically, we gradually become aware that these emotional and mental energies are something more than just fascinating but independent phenomena that have no meaning to the physical plane of life. In addition to being well organized and expressive at their own dimensions, the astral and mental worlds interact with each other—and with physical realities as well.

This interaction is of great significance to us, for there is a rich subtle counterpart to all of the physical forms of earth. Our books, homes, offices, and furniture all have astral and mental elements associated with them, as do geographical locations. So do words—as well as cultural traditions and personal habits. Even strong psychological patterns, such as obsessions and addictions, are rooted in astral and mental realities as well as in physical expression.

The physical forms we deal with are like containers for the inner forces associated with them. Like a battery, these "containers" can both absorb psychic energies and store them, so that they can be expressed at some later time. But like the battery, the physical forms of life are not the original source of the energies associated with them—merely a container that stores them.

Some people fail to appreciate this distinction. They treat physical forms and personal habits as though they were complete in and of themselves, rejecting the notion of any inner reality associated with tangible forms and expressions. But as a result, they end up interacting with just the superficial shells of life—the container, not the contents. Such people end up penalizing themselves tremendously as they struggle to make sense of life:

- They lack the awareness to comprehend the circumstances of life.
- They fail to grasp the larger context of the issues of life.
- They are overwhelmed by their reactiveness to conditions of physical life that are actually quite insignificant and could easily be controlled—forces such as fear or worry.
- They fail to understand how much of life could be controlled by them—if they had a better comprehension of the vast interaction of the subtle dimensions of life with the physical plane.

Examining the inner dimensions of the forms we deal with is therefore another important key to the full revelation of light through the psychic dimensions of life. It deserves to be a major part of our research and investigation.

All physical substance tends to soak up the dominant kinds of psychic energy expressed in conjunction with it. This process is very much like a swimming pool that absorbs heat from the sun and then slowly radiates it at night, as the temperature falls. But we must remember that the pool can also absorb impure elements—dirt and leaves and insects—which may make swimming less desirable unless they are periodically purged.

The walls and furnishings of our homes and offices absorb psychic energies in much the same way. During the day's activities, they soak up the dominant human expressions transpiring close by. When spouses argue, the walls hear it—and record it. When employees resent their work or hate their boss, the floor and ceiling absorb it—and the desks, too. When a pastor stirs up the fear of damnation, the pews register it. In bars, the dominant psychic patterns tend to be lust for drink and sexual activity. In nursing homes, a pall of despair generally builds up. Prisons are saturated by the criminal mentality and manipulativeness of the inmates. Many motel rooms reek of overheated sexuality. Discount stores are permeated by greed.

Not all of the psychic build-up in forms is negative,

of course. Some homes are havens of peace and harmony. It is often possible to discover areas of genuine devotion in monasteries and convents. The forces of faith and health may be exceptionally strong at a healing shrine. Music halls likewise can build up a tremendous atmosphere of harmony and inspiration, particularly after several centuries.

Whether noble or foul, these energies accumulate and become strong when the same kind of behavior is repeated on a daily basis, year after year. As a pattern strengthens, it begins to radiate the quality of the dominating energy throughout its space, affecting the people who continue to occupy it or use it.

When we buy a house, therefore, we are not just purchasing a physical structure. We are also buying the emotional and mental atmosphere which psychically pervades the home. If the home we buy became available as the result of a nasty divorce, for example, we are buying that couple's anger, jealousy, and suffering, as well as bricks and boards.

Even a casual visitor can be powerfully affected by the presence of these subtle patterns. A pilgrim to a shrine, for instance, may be healed and renewed by the blessings of a true religious site. Conversely, a business person may become depressed or irritated by the chaos encountered in an office he or she visits. Naturally, the impact is greatest on anyone who is actually immersed in the environment on a daily basis, not just an occasional visitor.

Not all people will be influenced by the psychic

dimensions of physical forms to the same degree. A crabby person will react to a crabby atmosphere just by giving in to it, whereas a more enlightened individual will be able to resist the temptation, even while wondering why he or she is suddenly so irritable. Nonetheless, both people are affected to a greater or lesser degree.

It is not just buildings that soak up psychic energies in this way, of course. All physical objects do, no matter how large or small. Solid personal objects tend to hold intimate, personal energies the longest—sometimes, thousands of years. This is especially true of jewelry and precious metals. Antique furniture also always brings with it a strong impression of the people who have owned it previously, as do antique automobiles. Often, the price of owning a piece of history is just not worth it—except in the case of prized musical instruments, which are often "attuned" to the musical genius of their earlier owners, thereby greatly enhancing their quality.

In a very real sense, any personal object becomes "haunted" by the presence of its owner or owners, and these patterns become an integral, important part of the object itself. The impact of such objects on our life may be enriching or distressing, but it is quite real and must be taken into account.

These dense physical objects are not the only forms that soak up psychic energies, however. Our psychological habits and cultural traditions—even the very forces that shape our daily thinking—do as well. We may not be accustomed to regarding habits and traditions as physical forms, but in truth they are. Our habits, routines, sense of identity, primary roles, and strong convictions all create patterns which are forms—and will soak up energy just as a chair might.

A good example of this phenomenon are people who must always be right. They put a strong emotional charge into winning every argument. Throughout the years, they have invested a lot of their self-esteem in being right—to the point where proving themselves right becomes an obsession, and robs them of their better judgment and self-restraint. They embarrass themselves by the way they attack others, magnify petty issues, and so on.

Such habits build up a strong "container" of righteousness and anger at psychic levels that radiates from these people on a constant basis, even when they are not engaged in disputations. It colors their thinking and their whole world view; to them, the art of conversation becomes nothing more than an opportunity for reasserting their superiority. And it psychically affects the thinking of anyone who comes close to them, even for a short period of time.

Another example would be people who are rigid in their political outlook. Having dedicated themselves to an arbitrary set of social theories, they are unable to understand current issues and political trends. They know what they know, and they charge up this attitude with periodic outbursts of anger and condemnation, as they demonize the opposition. They feast on their own indignation. Eventually, this process reaches the point of bigotry and malice. These people may talk about justice, dignity, and compassion, but as we examine the psychic elements of their beliefs and motives, it becomes clear that their true "ideals" are usually destruction and divisiveness.

The counterpoint to these sad examples would be professional musicians who get caught up in the thrall of their music every time they perform, creating a thoughtform that honors the piece of music, the composer, and their craft. Such musicians feed on the inner sustenance that has already built up around the piece they are performing—and enrich it themselves with their own insight, love, and genius.

Cultural, ethnic, and national groups likewise build repetitive patterns; instead of calling them habits, we refer to them as social traditions. As members of these groups pour their loyalty into customs and attitudes, these forms accumulate intense currents of psychic energy. Once formed, these traditions serve as reservoirs for vast amounts of psychic power, quietly influencing the behavior of group members and others who associate with them. It is this psychic energy within the forms of tradition that puts the "pressure" into "peer pressure."

How else can one explain the mob psychology that takes over and controls the behavior of thousands of people at sporting events, whipping them into a frenzy of fanaticism that few of them would display in their own affairs? Obviously, part of this frenzy becomes attached to the physical location of a stadium or arena—but another, far more mobile aspect of it is attached to the traditional desire of the group for victory.

Groups that feed on racial or gender bigotry demonstrate the same kind of "automatic pilot" behavior. Typically, these groups demand that their followers adhere strictly to the party line—and add to it a hostile "us versus them" mentality which blurs any genuine effort to think.

The same kind of pattern can be seen at work in the divisiveness that characterizes modern worker-management relationships. Union propaganda has created a demonic caricature of management that makes it virtually impossible for most union members to extend any sense of loyalty or dedication to their work. Their tie is to the union—not to the company that pays them their salary and guarantees their livelihood.

In each of these examples, the members of the group tend to lose personal control of their attitudes and behavior. They become automatons controlled by the bigotry and fanaticism of the group itself.

We do not traditionally think of patterns of bigotry and closedmindedness as interactions with the psychic world. But they are. What is worse, these patterns can build a tremendous intensity at inner levels without us ever knowing—unless we make the effort to explore these inner regions. The level of control they can exert over us as a result is enormous.

There are many ruts in which we can become stuck. The most powerful are not physical ruts at all. They are psychic ruts—habits and traditions that trap us in a particular obsession, fight, or cause, and keep us ensnared until we reawaken to the realities of life.

The question to ask ourself is, then: are we growing and evolving, responding to life and its opportunities? If so, we will explore life fully at each of its levels—psychically as well as physically—and act upon their rich potential as intelligently as we can. But if not, we may find ourself to be slowly sinking into the deadness of fixed beliefs and habitual reactions.

The moment we become a defender and protector of the status quo, rather than an agent of light and innovation, we are in jeopardy of being trapped by the boundaries we have defined for our life. We have determined our limits and surrendered to them.

If we are truly making an intelligent response to life, then it should be obvious that a single, fixed view of life is absurd and limiting, no matter how "correct" it may seem. The acceptance of an entrenched point of view leads quickly to the belief that there are no other acceptable options. Even worse, if we are inflexible about our beliefs, we will also probably have no interest in examining the larger picture which frames our limited views. As a result, our fixed perspective becomes like a figurative Frankenstein monster that comes back to threaten our freedom to learn and change—only we no longer remember that we created it!

Ultimately, the prototypical fixation is the belief that form is form and nothing more. Most people scorn the inner dimensions of forms as superstitious nonsense—simply because they do not yet possess the faculties to become aware of them. This kind of belief severely restricts their awareness of the inner dimensions of life—

and of the major forces that influence and affect them day by day. They become trapped in a one-dimensional system of thinking and understanding that cannot lead to wisdom, simply because it leaves out so much!

This trap paralyzes human thought both collectively and individually. At the individual level, the "thinker" stumbles on a tiny sliver of the truth and then fixates on it, refusing to grow and consider other fragments. This may be the fundamentalist who believes in interpreting the Bible literally, failing to realize that there are many layers of meaning associated with any great Biblical revelation. Or it might be a movement of social reformers trying to impose their coveted solution on the rest of society. In either case, it traps those who succumb to it in smallness and incompleteness. Their solutions and programs leave out too much to be able to work efficiently.

To break out of these traps, we must demolish our crystalized belief systems. We must recognize that we have focused our thinking so narrowly into our habits, traditions, and routines that we have, in essence, become trapped. We have stagnated. But instead of just recycling this stagnant energy, we must reconnect with the forces that can inspire and guide us. We need to embrace the realities of the inner life, using them to revitalize and renew our thinking.

In other words, we must develop the habit of always looking beyond the physical level of life, whether we are dealing with an object or building, a personal habit, or a cultural tradition. We must identify the emotional and mental forces interacting with the physical in this situation, shaping it and perhaps even limiting it. Then we must go beyond even these levels, and embrace the full relevance of this situation to the inner life.

We must begin working with the Big Picture.

In practice, there are a number of ways to launch this investigation.

One of the best is to wait until we are alone in a specific location, such as our office or home. If we can relax, we can then subjectively explore the inner dimensions of this space:

What kind of place is this? What is the dominant emotional tone? Is it happy—or depressing? Is it filled with the spirit of cooperation—or crackling with divisiveness? Would we enjoy staying here for any length of time? How would we describe the psychological tone of this place to someone else?

We must also evaluate the mental atmosphere: is it easy to concentrate and be innovative here? Or do new ideas get attacked by fear, jealousy, and smallmindedness the moment they are hatched? How have our ideas been shaped by the dominant mind set of this place?

At another time, we can review a strong conviction. How did we come to adopt this conviction? Is it the result of broadminded thinking? Or have we just fixated on our own experiences and preferences? Are we tolerant of other perspectives and opinions on this subject? How much psychological vigor do we derive from this conviction? Do we argue with others in order to make ourself feel better? Does this conviction help us interact with others—or close down doors? What greater principles influence this area of life? How can we expand our thinking to embrace these larger views?

We can likewise review a major role that we play automatically—parent, teacher, or whatever. How much have we defined our role based on our own evaluation of inner patterns and forces? How much have we just imitated pre-existing cultural patterns? Has this helped? How has it trapped us? How can we become more innovative in our role? What would it mean to fill this activity with wisdom, love, joy, or beauty?

The final stage of this exercise involves creating a specific thoughtform or seed thought that can be filled with light. Choosing a quality that we need to express in life or work—for example, patience, goodwill, joy, or harmony—we should project it through a primary phase of our work or life. We might, for example, imagine creating new lines of understanding and compassion with a difficult colleague.

Working with these exercises will provide practical experience in harnessing the psychic life within the forms of the world—a major part of the revelation of light on earth.

7.

The Psychic Bonds That Link Us

Few things in life are as powerful and as impressive as a mother's love for her child. As she holds the infant, nourishing, protecting, and watching over it, a strong bond of affection and goodwill is spun that connects the mother to the child. As the child grows up, this bond remains—nourishing, protecting, and watching over the offspring even when the mother can no longer be physically present to help the child.

This bond of affection is not just a show of maternal interest. It is a real and tangible connection—at psychic levels. It may be invisible physically, but this does not in any way diminish its importance. It remains an active channel for the expression of motherly love and concern, no matter how far apart mother and child might eventually be separated physically.

Such psychic bonds also exist outside of family relationships. Indeed, we are apt to have a strong, unbreakable bond with anyone with whom we have an important relationship—colleagues at work, friends, and neighbors, as well as with loved ones. But not all of these ties will be as benevolent as we would expect to find in the case of a mother and child.

Our psychic bonds are formed by our concern for others, either positive or negative. It is the intensity of the emotion expressed, not the quality of it, that determines the strength of the bond. For this reason, our hatred and contempt for an enemy will tend to create a far stronger bond—a leash, actually—than our sense of ease and companionship toward a friend. The sad truth is that we often invest far more energy and interest in sustaining negative bonds than in building healthy ones.

As this example suggests, our psychic ties are generated primarily by our emotions—and exist largely at the astral level. It is possible to build bonds at the mental level, of course, but few people control the emotions enough to be able to create relationships based on shared ideas and values, rather than likes and dislikes.

These bonds are two-way streets. In other words, if we treat others with courtesy, affection, and support, we can reasonably expect to receive similar treatment in return. Occasionally, we may encounter someone who spurns our helpfulness and rejects it with spite, scorn, or fear. But these instances will be in the minority—unless we also indulge in negative emotional expressions. If we tend to go through the day bitching and complaining, jealous of our colleagues, and grieving over our losses, others are apt to respond in kind.

In many instances, the dominant tone of any established psychic tie strongly colors the nature of our interaction. We may be determined to remain relaxed and detached while dealing with a cantankerous friend, but then find that we are unable to do so. We become reactive as always. What we are failing to realize is that the irritability within our established bond began stirring up our reactiveness even before we came into physical contact with him. We have let habitual annoyance assault us and provoke an immature, undisciplined reaction.

Our susceptibility to these established patterns of reaction is this great precisely because these bonds are psychic ties. They connect the tendencies, attitudes, and expectations within our subconscious with the subconsciouses of all of our friends, colleagues, and enemies. As such, these relationships remain active and interactive virtually all of the time, even when there is no direct physical contact.

Even though these elements of the relationship are invisible to us, they are extremely influential. We often try to hide our true emotions when dealing with others. But it is not possible to hide envy or contempt or other strong feelings at the astral level. They are as obvious as a flashing red light—and will be noticed quickly by the subconscious of the other person.

It is therefore of great importance to learn more

about these psychic bonds and how they affect our daily lives.

These psychic bonds exist—even if we are unwilling to admit to them. They are formed by the interaction of our own habitual patterns of emotional expression with the emotional feedback to us from others. If we treat an acquaintance with arrogance and superciliousness, for instance, it will probably draw a reaction of resentment and rebellion from the other person. Our emotion of arrogance mixes with a feedback of resentment to form a psychic bond of low quality that traps us both—until we learn to act with greater maturity. We need to replace our arrogance with respect and appreciation; he would need to replace resentment with tolerance and goodwill.

How strong are these bonds? They are indissoluble—until we take action to replace them with more noble psychic expressions. When intense, these bonds can last—and continue to influence us—for years and years after we break off physical contact with the other person. In fact, they can and do survive death of the physical body.

How much do these bonds control us? Far more than we imagine. It is quite possible to assume that we have completely healed a specific emotional wound, even when, at an unconscious level, elements of unresolved conflict still bind us psychically to the person or people originally involved. These untidy psychic bonds therefore continue to pose a threat to our psychological health, by sustaining an invisible connection to the anger, guilt, and fear in others.

It is also important to understand that the spectrum of these psychic bonds is a very broad one, indeed. A bond that is created through a moment's casual interaction with another person may well last for the rest of the day. A critical remark voiced only mentally regarding someone else's obnoxious behavior can easily expose us to instant psychic retaliation from the garbage in the other person's subconscious. We may not be able to shake off the damage until we have had a good night's sleep.

Just so, the impact of an intimate relationship can easily endure for as long as we continue to live—and longer—if it is not cleaned up. Divorced people who can neither forgive nor forget remain linked to their former spouses for years and years, their own angry reflections connecting them with the lingering resentment of the scorned partner.

We frequently encounter psychic dangers or conditions we never even begin to suspect. A sex-consumed person, for example, will send out tentacles of lust throughout a room as soon as he or she enters, trying to sense who may be responsive. Even if the tentacles pass us by, because we are nonresponsive, they leave an oddly slimy sensation that takes time—or conscious effort—to dissipate. Meanwhile, we are left wondering why wc have experienced a sudden upsurge in unpleasant sexual urges.

Any psychic bond with another person becomes magnified exponentially if the experience of sexual intimacy is added. Casual or recreational sex has become quite popular, because of the mistaken belief that it involves no commitment. Nothing could be further from the truth. Sexual intercourse links the partners psychically at many levels, with each partner taking on, to a startling degree, the inner, psychological and spiritual problems of the other. The act of sex results in a blending of the two subconsciouses in a way that is not easily disentangled. The mere fact that the partners have separated physically has little impact on the psychic state of the tie.

Obviously, this aspect of sex only becomes a problem if people abuse their sexual relationships. In a marriage based on mature love, wisdom, and commitment, the psychic dimensions of sex greatly enhance intimacy and caring. These dimensions only become a trap when sex becomes an undisciplined expression of self-gratification.

The same is true with all psychic bonds. Carefully created bonds can enhance every kind of relationship. In a therapy, for example, it is important for a therapist to establish a compassionate rapport with the patient. The therapist knows that the patient has real problems and suffering, but has no interest in reacting psychically to them. Instead, he focuses on patience, encouragement, and support, setting a tone of comfort and confidence for the client. If the patient responds with trust, the bond can become even more effective.

The same kind of tone can and should be established in every one of our relationships. The respect of a boss for his or her employees should kindle a reciprocal response of dedication and enthusiasm. The helpfulness of a person at work should inspire cooperation from colleagues.

The worst mistake we could make would be the attempt to solve problems of reactiveness simply by becoming indifferent—nonreactive to would-be friends and colleagues. A healthy person maintains strong, mature emotional bonds with the people in his or her life.

Fortunately, it is possible to gain control of these psychic bonds—at least from our end—both to reduce the negative impact of the wrong kind of bond and to utilize more effectively our natural ties as parent, friend, lover, or colleague. Until we make a conscious effort to seize control of these bonds, the process of psychic bonding will remain automatic. But even though it happens beyond the conscious knowledge of most people, this silent and invisible bonding can nonetheless cause great mischief. At the very least, it represents an opportunity for enrichment that we are failing to seize.

Before we can gain control of these bonds, however, we must clearly understand that the idea of psychic bonds is not just a clever metaphor. These bonds have a definite inner reality. They are made of emotional energy drawn from the substance of the astral plane and shaped into whatever quality suits the purpose of the emotions. In the case of one spouse who is possessive of the other, the bond may actually resemble a choke leash that can be yanked whenever the partner seems to wander too far. In contrast, the bond between two good friends might well resemble a continuous but invisible hug.

These bonds are made instantly in response to the

expression of a specific emotion toward another person—or group of people. If we become angry with a person, in other words, we fashion a bond of animosity which links us to that individual. The hatred in our emotions has been projected and attached to the astral body of the object of our ire.

Just so, if we shower a friend with blessings and goodwill in a quiet moment of prayer or meditation, we instantly establish a deep, more enriching bond with that individual. This, too, becomes attached to the emotional body of the other person, but in a way that liberates, instead of entrapping. The bond becomes a conduit for sharing more profound emotional qualities.

These bonds may also be established between individuals and groups. This is why it is often painful for a priest or nun to leave the Catholic Church; the process of disengaging from the psychic ties that bind them requires patience and goodwill. A similar but destructive phenomenon can be observed in the difficulty individual members often experience when trying to leave a cult or sect.

The key to regaining control of these bonds is to realize that they are part of our self-expression. These psychic energies emanate from our own continual emotional concern about the other person. And so, we can reclaim control—to disconnect the bond, if it is negative, or to strengthen and enrich it, if it is beneficial.

The first step toward disconnecting is to stop hating, lusting, regretting, and bitching. Taking this step involves a lot more than just restraining our emotions, however. We must also eliminate the underlying habits of judgmentalism, jealousy, desire, or rebelliousness that sustain our emotional behavior. We are not trying to shift our problem from an outer to an inner level; we are trying to replace it with something more wholesome.

To put this proposition even more bluntly, we need to learn to mind our own business. There is a price for sticking our nose into the affairs of others, and it is high in terms of psychic damage. We need to learn to "live and let live," keeping our curiosity directed toward the higher issues of life, not the pettiness of gossip and personal heartbreak that entertains so many people.

It may also be necessary to rein in any tendency toward too much sympathy for others, even when it is motivated by kindness. Whether it is a personal friend or the suffering millions that we sympathize with, the harmonious nature of sympathy tends to open a door emotionally that exposes us to all kinds of manipulation and silent coercion. We need to learn to keep this door closed, while responding to the suffering of life with compassion. Sympathy is often little more than a lamentation that draws attention to life's misery, whereas compassion is an expression of concern for fixing the underlying problem and eliminating the pain.

The second step, then, is to release our connection with the other person or group. Whatever their offense—or appeal—to us may have been, we release it to higher intelligence and universal justice. We withdraw our personal interest in the outcome, realizing that we cannot shoulder this burden for them.

Being unable to forgive a family member who has betrayed a promise is a good example. We need to understand that there are three issues involved: 1) the other person's betrayal of a commitment, 2) our anger about it, and 3) our stubborn refusal to forgive. Nothing can be done about the other person's betrayal, except to release him to the care of divine justice. But until we learn to forgive, we will perpetuate our ties to this problem—regardless of what he does! Forgiveness will not let the other person escape justice—but it will let us put this unfortunate event behind us and get on with our life.

Another example would be parents whose love for their children is far more possessive than it ought to be. As the children become adults, these parents are unwilling to let go. They insist on continuing to treat them as little kids. Such an attitude is certain to produce rebellion and anger, the fallout of which may endure for many years. This kind of parent needs to realize that their actions have been destructive; they need to develop more mature ways of expressing love, so that it does not interfere with the child's adulthood. They must detach themselves from their long-standing habit of wanting to control every facet of the lives of their children, releasing them to adulthood and the care of their own higher selves.

Taking action to regain control of these psychic bonds does not in any way imply that we are withdrawing from life, or becoming an emotional recluse. On the contrary, we are deliberately and intelligently detaching from the selfish levels of the emotions, refocusing our attention on the highest level of good—divine justice, goodwill, compassion, joy, and peace. We are becoming proactive in our ability to express spiritual forces to bless and to heal.

In short, we strive to be a charitable person, kindly in intent, patient and understanding in thought, and helpful and harmless in our behavior. We seek to transform ourself, like a compassionate parent who strives to guide and direct a willing but immature child.

A simple exercise can help us become aware of the inner dimensions of our ties with others. This can be done in a number of ways:

1. If we realize that we have become angry or resentful toward someone, we need to consider what kind of psychic darts they may be throwing at us in return. A headache, sense of guilt, a lowered self-image, or general confusion may all be signs that they are bombarding us with scorn, fear, or hate.

2. At meditative levels, we can reflect on a close friendship, dwelling on our affection and goodwill for this person. As this sense deepens, we should try to become aware of the response of goodwill and friendliness that comes to us psychically. We can then try to increase the quality and tone of our affection. Can we perceive a corresponding enrichment in the bond?

3. When watching a movie in a theater, or any time we are part of a large assembly, we can try to discern how much our reactions are influenced by the group of

strangers around us. Are we laughing at situations we normally do not find funny? Are we being sucked into a sea of sentimentality against our will? Are we being polluted by the lust for violence? As we discover ties of this nature, we need to make the effort to think for ourself, so that we can enjoy the performance without this kind of distortion. Above all, we must be sure not to carry these casual ties home with us. We need to leave them in the theater!

4. Another key to understanding these ties is to work meditatively to repair or enrich an existing relationship. This work begins by gently reviewing the aspects we dislike or disapprove of—and how they shrink in significance as we consider them with tolerance, patience, and understanding. Next, we must review the many aspects of this person that we admire and respect, energizing them with our gratitude, appreciation, and even reverence for their inner spiritual design.

5. We can also work in this way to repair or enrich our bond with a group of people—ethnic, racial, religious, or political. Follow the same procedure as in step four.

No doubt we will meet with some internal resistance as we seek to break these psychic bonds. We must therefore remain mindful that the higher self will always support any effort to redeem our psychic bonds.

8.

The Dimming of the Light

There are many treasures of light and love awaiting us, whenever we prove ourselves ready to become a prospector of the divine—to shift at least some of our attention away from the physical spectacles of life and explore the rich vastness of the inner worlds. At the same time, however, it would be a major error to assume that any and all efforts to explore the psychic worlds will lead automatically to a glorious revelation of light. It all depends upon who we are, our point of departure, and our intentions.

In this sense, our quest is not unlike that of those explorers who roamed throughout America in hope of finding a fabled city of gold. If they did not have the internal fortitude to withstand the rigors of exploration, or had only a vague idea of which regions to investigate, they would fail, no matter how energetically they proceeded—or how much they believed in their venture.

In exploring the psychic realms of life, we are traveling inward, not westward. The obstacles we are apt to face, therefore, are not external ones. They will be found within ourselves. If, for example, we happen to be a crabby, fearful, or gloomy person, our negativity will strongly resonate with similar elements in the psychic worlds, drawing us to them. Instead of discovering light or love, we will find ourselves in a pit of meanness, terror, or despair—hardly a propitious beginning to what ought to be an exciting adventure.

Most of us probably think that our customary focus of attention is of the very highest level. But is it? It may very well be uncluttered at conscious levels, but what is the dominant subconscious tone of our thoughts and feelings, our beliefs and expectations? What is the baseline of our focus of attention? Answering these questions is the first step the would-be explorer of the psychic dimensions of life should make on his journey of exploration.

If, for instance, we believe that the world is rotten, we probably also believe that all politicians are crooks, all business people are unethical, our neighbors cannot be trusted, and life has treated us unfairly. This kind of cynical attitude toward life may seem to work adequately as we interact with others on the physical plane, but it will definintely skew the way we explore the inner dimensions of life. Cynicism acts as a filter that screens out everything which would contradict it—in other words, everything noble, beautiful, and divine—and draws to us a heightened dose of our own medicine—negativity, hostility, and gloominess.

Habitual attitudes of worry, guilt, or fear will affect us in exactly the same way, by screening out the nurturing qualities of life and magnetically drawing us to unredeemed forces of threat, confusion, and disaster.

Such habitual patterns become the lenses through which we perceive and interact with physical life. A woman who thinks all men are bums is incapable of establishing a constructive relationship with any man, no matter how caring and sensitive he may be. Her attitude dooms her to cycle after cycle of disappointment and frustration—not because men are bums, but simply because she perceives them in this light!

Before we can explore the psychic worlds, we must clearly understand that these same habitual attitudes likewise act as the lenses through which we will investigate and discover the inner side of life. If our attitudes and perspectives on life fill us with inspiration and hope, they will lead us safely to the discovery of the light within us. But as long as they remain polluted by negative stereotypes and immature urges, they will cause mischief in our life.

These are the forces that lead to the dimming of the light, not just within ourself but also within the whole of society. When more than one person shares fear or despair, it becomes a mutual blight. If a large segment of a group or society share it, it becomes a collective poison.

The widespread epidemics of pessimism, fear, and anxiety in the world testify starkly to the need for more and more people to confront this problem within their own lives—and heal it! Seldom has the light within the world circle of humanity flickered more dimly than it does today. We have come to the brink of estrangement—from one another, and, even worse, from God.

And yet, seldom has there been greater potential for individuals to make a significant contribution toward ending this steady dimming of the light. As each of us learns to reverse this process of alienation within ourselves, we help society learn to reverse it on its larger scale.

Indeed, this is a major part of our work as children of God.

To join in the labor of reversing the dimming of the light, we must understand that it is our habitual thoughts and attitudes that set the tone of our outlook, not our peak thoughts, as might be attained in prayer or meditation. Peak spiritual thoughts can become an important ingredient in this effort, but only as we learn to integrate them into our habitual baseline of thought and attitude.

Far too often, this integration does not occur. We revisit a painful memory—but fail to heal it. We feel the pain once more, but do nothing to neutralize it. We brood on the scheming and plotting that is going on at the office—and soon find ourselves scheming and plotting how to get even. We dwell on the injustice in our world—yet do nothing to overcome the harm we have experienced. We feel sorry for ourselves and the burden we must carry—and forget to rejoice in the part of our life that is working. We relish the latest tidbits of scandal and gossip, either in Washington or Hollywood—without appreciating that most people live successful lives of decency and achievement.

No one forces us to carry this kind of baggage around with us—we do it all on our own. Nor should we make the mistake of shrugging and saying, "It's just human nature." These attitudes are no more part of human nature than being sick with the flu is. They are the pathologies of human nature, not inherent qualities of it.

The accumulated burden of our wounded feelings—pessimism, gloom, fear, guilt, and worry—must be approached in exactly the same manner. In each case, we need to learn that the negative mood severely restricts our ability to explore the inner levels of life—and then work to eliminate it from our psychological makeup, replacing it with a healthier, more spiritual quality—a quality that embodies the light of life.

Until we become alarmed by this danger, we will remain trapped in an earthbound personality which will inevitably distort our perceptions about the meaning of daily life—and likewise skew our impressions as we try to extend our awareness and explore the psychic realms of life. We will greatly cripple our efforts.

It is important to understand the heavy penalty paid by anyone who participates in the dimming of the light, either within themselves or within society. A lot of attention, for instance, has been given to the problem of abuse in recent years. Unfortunately, the typical approach to this problem is to agonize over past abuse, without healing it. Instead of activating forgiveness and insight, most individuals just create a victim consciousness that portrays themselves in terms of pain and suffering. In this way, such individuals not only isolate themselves from real solutions, by rooting themselves in suffering and misery, but also add to their problems, by resonating with powerful flows of negativity from unredeemed levels of the psychic worlds.

If such people were to set out on a quest of the inner worlds, the only regions they would be capable of exploring would be those that would support their self-pity and suffering—those regions of the astral plane that are typically referred to as "hell" or the "underworld" by most major world religions! The spiritual and divine regions of the inner worlds would be closed to them—by their own acts.

It may seem odd that the accumulation of bad memories and attitudes can have such a powerful impact, but it is just a simple matter of cause and effect. It is like the lady who daily throws her garbage into her backyard. The yard is fenced, so she cannot see the trash. She stays indoors, so she cannot smell it. But the pile—and its resulting odor—grow stronger, even though she remains unaware of them.

Our personal feelings are fed by invisible psychic forces. These forces may be toxic or nurturing—it all depends on the quality of our feelings. If they are toxic, as they commonly are, they will grow in noxiousness, just as the odor of the lady's garbage pile grows. If, in addition, we spend time actively stirring up the stench, the toxicity multiplies all the more rapidly.

In other words, every time we lose our temper, we stir up the stench. Every time we worry, we pollute our outlook. Every time we protest the unfairness of life, we foul ourselves.

Imagine if everyone in the neighborhood behaved the same way! What a horror! Yet this is precisely what happens every day at the astral level of mass consciousness. Each of us tosses our share of anger, grief, and worry onto the collective pit of psychorubble. Unfortunately, this creates conditions on the astral plane far worse than smog in any major city in the world.

On top of this, as large numbers of the media, politicians, and citizens become shocked and outraged by the conditions of life, they once again stir up the miasma of this stench. Our entire culture becomes polluted—and each of us is affected as well, as we strive to exist within an increasingly toxic atmosphere. It makes it far more difficult for any one of us to think clearly—or to respond effectively to the light within us.

Sadly, the light of our society and culture has become so dimmed that most modern philosophers, politicians, and theologians just assume that we must endure this decline. Many psychologists, for example, view anger and depression as normal, natural aspects of living. To their way of thinking, we do not need to heal anger or depression—just learn how to express it well! These same experts also believe that only behavior can be changed, not human character. This illustrates how completely their views have been infected by despair and gloom and the light of their imagination dimmed.

Just so, we have all neglected our duty to transcend gloom and negativity. Some political thinkers, for example, assert that both crime and poverty are caused by exploitative and oppressive forces in society. This is a sign that they have allowed paranoia and envy to color their thinking to the point where their capacity to make sense of life has been crippled.

Likewise, the current focus in public education of replacing the goal of excellence with lower minimum standards has greatly diminished education. The resulting slide in the quality of education has generated a momentum that must be halted.

Can the momentum be reversed? Of course. Will it be easy? Of course not. The difficulty lies in the fact that the lens of negative attitudes creates a vicious loop. Intolerant people find more evidence to support their anger than they do to support life's benevolence. Victims find recurring reasons to continue being discouraged, instead of finding solutions to their problems. They create a repetitive focus of thought and feeling that highlights their special suffering—which excludes all other perspectives, and most of the light of the inner worlds.

Were it not for the momentum of psychic energy

that can be built up in these narrowly focused, self-destructive habits of negativity and doom, it might be relatively easy to change them, both individually and in society. But because so much of the force we have invested in these habits is psychic, and not physical, we cannot just "pull the plug." Instead, we must build up healthy forms of self-expression.

In short, we must cultivate expressions of the light.

We must begin to express optimism instead of despair.

We must begin to express goodwill instead of resentment.

We must express cooperation instead of distrust.

We must express confidence instead of fear.

But first, we need to identify the closed loops of negativity in our own attitudes and perspectives. If the memory of some event always reproduces pain, replaying this memory may only confirm the severity of our wounds, and reinforce the pain. This connection is a closed loop.

These closed loops are the mechanism that perpetuates the status quo and cripples our potential to grow. But just being aware that we have these closed loops is not enough; we need the power to break the loops permanently.

This power comes from the will to change. We must become not just determined, but also deeply committed to the changes we are making.

As always, the focus must be on ourself. We cannot wait for society to change or for government to act. We must take action within ourself. If we are caught in a loop of gloom, we must take action to find and express joy within our life—and then within society. If we have been trapped in a loop of anxiety and worry, we must take action to cultivate serenity within ourself—and then make peace with others, with our work, and with our expectations about society.

Once we harness the light within us to break even one of these loops, it will become a continuing source of renewal and transformation—clearing our outlook so we can view life more constructively, more charitably, and more abundantly. As we harness the light repeatedly, our attitudes and perspectives will change. So will our sense of identity, our values, and our beliefs. Slowly, subtly, even our character, as well as our behavior, will be altered. We will start to express the light. It is only when we can express the light in this way that the exploration of the psychic dimensions of life can proceed safely.

As we make these changes, we stop being part of the problem and become part of the solution. We become a positive influence on the psychic dimensions of life.

Our optimism opens a door to higher possibilities.

Our joy attracts us to a more abundant life.

Our confidence initiates us into a more productive life.

We can explore these loops—and their connections with the inner planes—through a simple exercise of self-examination. We begin by picking one of the following to review: gloom, anger, self-doubt, fear, or self-pity. We can then ask ourselves how we should explore a satisfactory alternative to this negative condition.

What evidence can we find to justify a healthy change in behavior?

Have we stifled change—for example, by being obsessed with the fear of failing?

Where can we best begin making improvements?

How has this negative attitude been magnified by other bad habits—such as a habit of ruminating on our darkest experiences?

What mind sets or attitudes have been a toxic influence on us? What can we do about them?

Where are we already expressing positive attitudes in our life? How can we expand them so they can help integrate the life of spirit into our daily life?

How can we draw the darkness into the light, thereby transforming it?

How can we become more tolerant or supportive in our behavior, so that the negativity is forced out of our self-expression?

How can we expand this work to transform the negativity in others—or in society? How can we inspire others to join us in our exploration of the treasures of the inner life?

In this short exercise lies the key to expanding awareness throughout the psychic dimensions of life. This is how we can reverse the darkening of the light, so that it shines forth anew with vitality and purpose.

9.

The Laws of Psychic Activity

One of the great developments of the last two hundred years has been the emergence of electricity as a practical source of energy. We now accept electricity as commonplace, taking it so much for granted that we only realize how much we rely on it when a power outage occurs.

Electricity was not invented; the earth itself is a charged electrical object. It has always been available to humanity for its use. Why then did we not tap into this enormous source of power earlier?

The answer is simple: we did not know about electricity's vast potential for serving our needs. We did not understand it. But beginning in the mid-eighteenth century, the scientific community began to take a serious interest in this phenomenon. It started exploring the laws and principles that regulate its actions, transmission, and use. One of these scientists, Benjamin Franklin, was delving into the nature of electricity when he conducted his famous experiment of flying a kite during a thunderstorm. A direct result of his work was the invention of the lightning rod, which has protected farms and homes from lightning strikes ever since.

Electricity is a tremendous asset to human living. But it does behave along very precise principles and laws. A person who fails to learn these laws or respect them runs the risk of suffering a severe shock. But a knowledgeable person can work with electricity with no danger at all—can even run electrical currents through his body and light up a bulb being held in his hand, if he knows as much about electricity as Nikola Tesla did.

Much the same is true of psychic energies. Most of humanity is as much in the dark about their psychic connections as they were about electricity two hundred years ago. But the whole planet exists within a psychic energy field—several of them, in fact. Our discovery of these energies can open the door to whole new sources of power and insight, with many practical applications. But before we try to develop any measure of psychic sensitivity, we need to learn the laws and principles governing these energies—how they work, how they interconnect us, and how they can best be developed. If we fail to understand these laws, we may well receive as much of a shock as we might from touching a live wire.

In this regard, there are a number of laws to explore.

Our focus of attention directs energy, and energy follows our focus. Our consciousness is the means by which we interact with psychic energies. As we focus our attention on any idea, person, or object, we immediately begin to interact with its psychic dimensions. We impress energies upon it psychically, and in turn receive impressions from it psychically.

Some people might wonder: if this is true, why am I not aware of these impressions? The answer may be surprising: we are aware of these impressions—we just do not understand their significance.

Anyone who has ever worried demonstrates this law. If we brood on our misery, we focus our attention on what is wrong about life. This in turn draws to us free-floating energies of misery and depression, and our basic mood snowballs. If we brood on someone else's misery, the same result will ensue. This is one of the problems of unskilled psychic activity. If we tune into someone with serious emotional problems, do we have enough detachment to prevent us from being caught up in their depression, anger, bitterness, or fear?

The same problem can occur on a global basis as well. If we dwell even to a small degree on the apparent hopelessness of our situation, it will trigger within us a psychic response to *Weltschmerz,* the overwhelming sense of global suffering and pain in mass consciousness.

By the same token, a steady expression of gratitude toward the soul and the constructive aspects of life focuses our attention on the supportive, generous nature of the light within us. It builds a psychic receptivity which attracts support and help far more readily than would otherwise occur, whenever it is needed.

The implications of this law to psychic development are immense. To become receptive to impressions, we must attune our consciousness to the proper source, and learn to stay focused in our attentiveness until we have fully received the message, insight, or attribute that is being impressed upon us.

All psychic energies are magnetic. Emotions and thoughts are living energies that act magnetically. They attract feelings, ideas, and inspirations that are of a similar wavelength. Anger attracts more anger. Grief attracts further grief. A new idea will attract corollaries that support it. An inspiration will attract opportunities to apply it.

It is this principle that makes it possible to start a creative project with just a glimpse of an idea. As we focus our attention on working out the details, additional impressions swarm into our head, fleshing out the outline.

It is also this principle that underscores the importance of thorough mental housecleaning before undertaking psychic work. If our emotions are filled with bitterness and hopelessness and our mind is laced with pessimism, the psychic impressions we attract will be skewed toward doom and condemnation. We will tend to concentrate on the darkest elements in other people, in projects, and in society, coloring the information we glean.

Exercising an attitude, habit, or skill increases its strength. Excessive brooding increases our resentment toward life. A steady expression of gratitude, on the other hand, builds a wholesome aura of appreciation for excellence and respect for others.

This principle explains the foolishness of any excessive preoccupation with the problems of the past. The more we relive the past tragedies of our life, either on an analyst's couch or in our own imagination, the stronger and more rooted in our subconscious these memories become. Conversely, the more we de-emphasize the importance of these memories, the weaker they become.

One of the biggest problems with developing psychic awareness is that we remain trapped by any excessively strong negative pattern in our subconscious, preventing us from becoming receptive to external impressions. Some of the most common of these traps are fear (especially fear of the unknown), anxiety, resentment, intolerance, depression, and grief.

The key to eliminating these problems is the practice of detachment.

All psychic energies are highly infectious. The energies of life are constantly in movement. If we are beset with gloom and depression, these emotions instantly blight all life forms close by, and continue to do so as long as we sustain these feelings. Over a long period of time, this impact might be enough to kill plants, make pets neurotic, and poison the consciousness of other family members, colleagues, or clients we work with regularly.

On the other hand, courage and joy can be just as contagious, but in a helpful, uplifting way. Nothing can lift a person out of a slough of depression faster than the joyfulness of spirit.

The same effect on motivation and ambition can be observed in the presence of a strong will to achieve—such as the power of Sir Winston Churchill to rally the people of Britain during the dark days of World War II.

This law applies to the development of psychic skills in numerous ways. One important one is that intuition is actually a natural form of human communication. We send and receive psychically at all times. To do either effectively, we must just make sure that the signal is strong enough—by focusing carefully on the act of sending or receiving an impression.

It also implies that we must proceed with care in developing psychic skills, lest we be overwhelmed by the anger or strong thoughts of a person close to us.

The subconscious receives and reacts automatically, with or without our conscious awareness. The human subconscious receives and reacts to virtually every impression it encounters, whether it is obvious to us or not. In reading a book, for example, the subconscious will register the full impact of the thoughtform surrounding the text, even though our conscious mind only reads the literal words. While driving downtown, our subconscious will register the thoughts and feelings of our spouse at home, even though we are not in direct contact.

These impressions are registered automatically,

whether we are psychic or not. As we learn to recognize psychic impressions, however, more of these impacting thoughts and feelings will begin to well up into our conscious recognition.

The inner becomes the outer. All inner energies and patterns eventually express themselves at outer levels. A mental value begins to shape our attitudes and character, and eventually is expressed through our behavior. A pattern of resentment ultimately irritates the physical body.

Just so, any dominant quality existing at unconscious levels will eventually control outer behavior. Some people try to handle a difficult trauma by simply becoming indifferent to it. They pretend it does not exist any longer. If necessary, they will shove the entire memory pattern out of the subconscious, so that it exists only at unconscious levels. For a long period of time, the suppressed memory seems to cease bothering the individual. But eventually, the pressure of the memory begins to seep back in. It regains control of character and behavior, even though the memory still cannot be consciously recalled. The psychic force of the pattern pops out of its restraint.

This principle illustrates the need to approach psychic unfoldment as the development of consciousness, not just as a set of gimmicks or tricks to be acquired. We are not learning telepathy, in other words; we are learning the art of awareness. We are not learning clairvoyance; we are learning to see reality. As we peel back the veils that have kept us from perceiving the psychic levels of life, we may well have to make major adjustments in our self-control and self-understanding. We may have to heal major conflicts or schisms within our consciousness. It is easiest to make these adjustments if we anticipate them, instead of letting ourself be trapped in hidden problems.

Psychic energies are transformed by drawing them into a higher force. Anger can only be healed by transforming it with the spiritual force of goodwill and tolerance. We need to understand that anger is an inappropriate response to a person, event, or condition. It is polluting our mechanism of perception—our ability to perceive the psychic dimensions of life. It magnetically attracts us to other angry people, inducing a downward spiral toward more intense anger. To reverse this self-defeating process, we must focus our attention on the compassion and tolerance of spirit, flooding our attitudes toward this other person, event, or condition with these forces until we are released from the feeling of anger. We must continue repeating this saturation of our consciousness with goodwill and tolerance until all traces of anger are removed.

The same procedure can be used to cleanse traces of grief, despair, hate, envy, or anxiety. All of these emotional patterns clog and distort any effort we might make to become psychic.

Control of each kind of psychic energy lies in the next more subtle dimension of life. Our feelings are controlled by the disciplined mind. Our values and thoughts are disciplined by the ideal and design of the soul. With each step we take toward greater self-control in this manner, we therefore open up the ability to operate consciously at a more refined level of perception and impression.

Most psychic perception being registered today operates only at the astral level, through the emotions. As a result, it tends be personal and erratic. Its range and perspective is highly limited and prone to distortion.

The psychic awareness that can be cultivated at the level of the mind is far more objective, detached, and accurate. The range of perception also extends much further into the future. This mental level of awareness allows us to deal with a far greater number of impressions simultaneously.

The ability to register intuitive impressions, working at the level of the soul, is an even more powerful and accurate type of awareness. It allows the individual to identify with the consciousness within other forms, not just their superficial feelings and sensations.

As we reflect on these laws and principles, we begin to understand that we can create a lot of mischief for ourself (and our family and friends) if we do not proceed correctly in cultivating psychic skills. It is not the intent of these laws and principles to limit our awareness or abilities in any way; the laws and precepts give us a structure that will let us explore the psychic dimensions of life safely and productively.

A good exercise to put these laws to work for us, therefore, could begin by asking the following questions:

Do we control our moods, or let our moods control us? The answer to this question will indicate whether or not we are ready to begin exploring the psychic worlds.

Do we complain about what's wrong in life more than we praise and express gratitude for what is right? The idea in exploring this question is to determine how we normally focus our attention. Is it focused on everything that is supporting our efforts—especially the soul? If it is, then our focus of attention will be receptive to all kinds of benevolent psychic influences. Or is it focused on our problems and suffering? Do we wallow regularly in self-pity and worry? If we do, then our focus of attention has been captured by a repeating cycle of self-abuse.

Do we nurse hurts and grievances more than we nurture our friendships? Most humans have a tendency to dwell on the few traits or attitudes in their friends that offend them, rather than reflect periodically on the good qualities they admire in these people. This focus of attention magnetizes their own consciousness to hostility, suspicion, and mistrust. As a result, when they try to develop psychically, the first impressions they react to are often the cruelty, fear, and worry in others.

What guides us? Are our values and principles based on the best within us—or do we take our cues from mass consciousness and the ways of the world? Are we guided by ethnic traditions? Are we dominated by our wishes for money, our dreams for romance, our desire for power, or our fantasies about great magical prowess? Or are we inspired by spiritual ideals?

How do we invoke ideas? When we need understanding or inspiration, at what level do we seek them? At the level of physical life? The emotional plane? The realm of the mind? Or at the level of archetypal thought? If we focus our attention on drawing our inspiration and understanding from divine archetypes, we will safely build durable psychic skills.

Do we make a regular attempt to align ourself with the spiritual will? The spiritual will represents the force of the intent of the soul. Are we motivated by this spiritual will—or by our desires, wishes, and petty wants? Do we invoke the power of the will to expand our control and authority over selfish feelings and urges?

Are we attuned to the ideal of harmony? Do our actions deepen schisms and conflicts, or do we promote cooperation and healing wherever trouble arises? If violence and bad taste have a secret appeal to us, it is going to be very hard to develop an enlightened use of psychic abilities.

Are we in tune with divine life? The ultimate goal of any intuitive exploration of life should be to operate on the wavelength of the divine Plan. Intuitive explorations should bring us closer to the heart and mind of spirit. If they estrange us, then we are not implementing the laws and principles enunciated here.

10.

Invisible Friends

All of us have many friends. Most of these friends live close to us, or work with us, and so we see them frequently. But others are friends we made in school, or years gone by, or other places. We keep in touch with them by letters, telephone calls, and perhaps even the internet, but we rarely if ever see them in person. Nevertheless, the lack of physical contact does not diminish the strength of our ties of friendship—or our ability to communicate effectively with them. They are, in effect, invisible to us, but we are able to compensate quite satisfactorily for their invisibility.

Other people are invisible to us as well, but we do not always do as good a job compensating for their apparent lack of presence in our lives. These are people we have known earlier in this lifetime, but who have died—or people we knew before we incarnated, but who stayed "behind" in the inner life while we took on the dense shell of a physical body.

These people are every bit as much alive as we are, except that they lack a physical body. They have a personality with emotions and a mind just as we do. As we expand our own abilities to be aware psychically and to communicate telepathically, we discover that they have the same abilities—and these skills are already well developed! It is therefore possible to communicate with them, even though they remain invisible to us. The process differs little from using a telephone, except that the entire conversation occurs within our own mind.

In spite of popular fears and beliefs, our friendships are not interrupted by death—or even by birth. The bond of affection and respect we develop with a close friend or loved one continues to link us without interruption even if the other person dies. Just so, similar bonds continue to link us with close friends we leave behind us on the inner realms when we begin a new life.

Our need for friendship is one of the strongest drives in the human experience. We value the common sense, guidance, and wisdom close friends feel free to give us. We appreciate the support and encouragement these companions lend when we run into obstacles or crises. We cherish the fellowship we derive from being with a circle of close friends.

It is sad that most humans give up conscious interaction with friends for long passages of time, just because death—or birth—has made them invisible to us. It is equally unfortunate that most physical people never go to the trouble of attracting new potential friends from the inner levels of life, even though such individuals could immensely enrich their lives.

Indeed, rediscovering the vast contingent of invisible friends that we can contact is one of the first fruits and true joys of the process of developing psychic skills. We soon learn that these old and dear friends have always been a presence in our life—we just were not aware of them! If they are invisible, it is only in our own perception. We have never been invisible to them.

Who are these invisible people—and why are they part of our life? They are human beings who once had a physical body but happen to be without one at the present moment. They are not angels or archangels, in spite of the tendency of some people to refer to them as "guardian angels." They are thoroughly human. Nor are they demons, in spite of the tendency of other people to denounce communication with invisible people as the work of the devil. How can it be the work of the devil to exchange ideas and love with friends and family?

Nor is the ability to communicate with invisible people forbidden by any religion. The fundamentalists who oppose these communications are a) misreading the Bible, and b) failing to understand what they condemn. The book of Acts, in fact, explicitly encourages such communication, and it was a common practice among early Christians. The pursuit of our highest good is always a noble enterprise, regardless of what smallminded people profess.

The invisible people who come to us first as we develop psychic responsiveness are long-time friends. They like us and care for us. They have been a part of our life for a long time; now we are becoming aware of this fact. They will become as much a part of our life as we will allow. As with any friend, it is always up to us how much we trust our invisible friends, how well we get to know them, and how much we interact with them.

It is important to remember, however, that they are friends, nothing more, nothing less. They are not slaves whom we can command as though they were invisible valets. Such an attitude would quickly repel any intelligent person, invisible or not. Nor are they "guides" or "masters." They care for us and support the best within us, but they are not all-knowing or all-seeing. They are fellow companions on our spiritual journey. We are not meant to become dependent upon them.

As we communicate with them, therefore, we should listen with respect and friendship, but we should not automatically accept any idea or "message" that pops into our head. Invisible friends will never deliberately mislead us, but they can be as mistaken as we can be. In addition, there always exists the potential that we may distort their messages and ideas as we register them, in order to make them consistent with our own wish life or feelings.

As we get to know these people well, our relationship will mature. When appropriate, they may feel free to criticize our actions or jog our conscience. In so doing, they are just behaving as any good physical friend would behave, if it became clear that we were foolishly heading in a wrong direction.

There are numerous ways we can benefit from developing a conscious communication with our invisible friends. A physical friend might help us move or lend a hand with a remodeling project. Just so, an invisible friend might help us remodel our mental household, by pointing out our need to overcome certain fears or our need to rein in our anger and hostility. Our invisible friends live at a level of consciousness where our subconscious is tangible and easily explored. A tendency to distort the helpful suggestions of others, therefore, would be an objective fact to them, even though we might be completely blind to it. A habit of dishonesty or self-deception would be as tangible to such people as a big nose would be to us. As a result, they can alert us to major problems in the subconscious that might sabotage our best interests if they were allowed to go uncorrected.

In this regard, however, it is important to note that our invisible friends will not lift a finger to do the work of cleaning up our subconscious for us. If we initiate the proper work and see it through, they will support us wholeheartedly. But if we ignore the mess at hand, they will not clean it up for us! They will just become less interested in trying to help us.

Invisible friends can also help us master basic life

skills. As we invoke the next step in our growth, they can help open our eyes to the opportunities that will best nurture and serve this growth. They can also help enhance our ability to perform any skillful activity, such as athletics, music, schoolwork, or our work. A pianist, for example, would attract invisible musicians who would provide new insights and possibilities in playing that instrument. An author would get help in developing characterizations and plots. A surgeon might get suggestions for adapting a procedure for the needs of a specific patient.

These people will also be very responsive to specific requests. An author who was stumped as to how to proceed, for example, might turn inwardly to his writing friends and ask: "Well, how would you do it?" If he were receptive, the answer would come back faster than a synapse can relapse. Another person, having just been let go from a job, might ask for help in understanding the larger reasons and designs behind this turn of events. Once again, his invisible friends would be more than happy to oblige.

Occasionally, an invisible friend may even ask us to help in a creative project he or she is sponsoring! As strange as this proposition may seem at first, we need to understand that invisible people are just as involved in life on earth as we are. They belong to this planet as much as we do. They are involved in helping society develop just as much as we are. It is quite natural for them to have projects to oversee—and to ask for our cooperation and assistance.

Beyond this, our invisible friends can also help us attune more effectively to the life of spirit. They will not make this attunement for us, of course, but they can help. In this regard, it is also important to remember that chatting telepathically with an invisible friend is not the same as contacting spirit. Attunement to spirit is a process of integrating our own thoughts, feelings, and motives with the designs, love, and intent of our own higher self.

And so, even though it would be ludicrous to expect our invisible friends to meditate for us, they can facilitate our efforts to meditate and pray. They can help us become calm and centered. They can help us gain insight into the changes occurring within us. They can show us the relationship between the events and crises in our life and our pleas for help in growing. They can be an enormous help in exploring the inner realms of life. And when we are exhausted, they can help connect us to inner sources of energy to restore our perspective and alertness.

In addition to assistance of this kind, our invisible friends can also help protect us from our own negativity—our own irritability, anger, or fear. When given permission, they will not hesitate to interact with us in such a way that we begin to discover how destructive some of these emotions can be.

At other times, they can be a solid source of comfort and support, as they help us focus in the peace and detachment of our higher self, enabling us to renew our dedication to the best within us.

Most of all, however, they can teach us the meaning of friendship—and help us strengthen the bonds of companionship we enjoy with physical people. They enrich our celebrations and triumphs and teach us that joy is one of the great hallmarks of spirit.

Communication with invisible friends develops as we learn the basic principles of psychic responsiveness in general. Our subconscious is aware of all kinds of stimuli that impinge upon it constantly. Some of these stimuli arrive through our physical senses; some are picked up from the feelings of people close to us and mass consciousness. Other, more refined input comes from our higher mind and our higher self in the form of guidance, love, and inspiration. The art of becoming psychic lies in learning to recognize these various forms of input, turning up the volume on the subtle stimuli of the higher mind and self while turning down the noise of the coarser stimuli of the emotions and mass consciousness.

As we learn to respond to the more subtle whispers of the higher mind and self, we also become aware of the gentle input of invisible friends. This input rarely comes as a voice that we hear as tangibly as a chime or bell; it is more of a mind-to-mind contact. Their thoughts and messages emerge in the midst of our own thoughts and reflections. At first, in fact, we are apt to believe that they are just our own thoughts and ideas. But as we listen more carefully, we begin to recognize that they come from someone other than ourself.

Since both ends of this communication occur within our own awareness, it is easy to jump to the erroneous conclusion that we are just making it all up. But this would be unfortunate, for it would lead us to discount a valuable friendship. We need to realize that even though the thoughts are occurring within our own mind, they are being prompted by the ideas of our invisible friends. The ideas have come from them, even though they are now arising in our awareness. It is almost as if we are reading from invisible cue cards.

An unexpected shift in mood or understanding is often one of the best indicators that we have been communicating with an invisible friend. If we have been discouraged by recent events, and then suddenly register an insight that revives us with optimism and hope, it is likely that we have opened our mind just enough to let one of our friends from the inner side of life slip in a measure of wisdom and cheerfulness.

One of the easiest ways to improve our responsiveness to our friends is to take more time to think about them in a speculative, wondering fashion. If we are planning a new project, for example, we might take the time to ask: "I wonder how my invisible friends would approach this project?" The query will invite their input and give them permission to influence our speculations and lead us toward productive ideas. Asking the right questions is the best way to set up this link.

Even those of us who are not consciously psychic can receive information from invisible friends; the process is just a bit more cumbersome. In such cases, invisible friends respond to needs by subtly altering our focus of attention and degree of interest. If we are trying to make a career decision, for instance, one choice will repeatedly come to the fore and dominate our attention, until we accept it as our decision. We have no inkling that we have been conversing with an invisible being; we just assume that we have had a brilliant hunch of our own.

There are, of course, a few common sense limitations and precautions which need to be observed in communicating with invisible friends—or even physical ones.

First, invisible friends are not interested in doing our work for us. We are still responsible for making decisions and pursuing our own maturity. We must take charge of our own growth and productivity.

Second, invisible friends are not a substitute for spirit. While they can loosely be considered "spirit entities," they are not spirit in the sense of the soul and the life of the divine. It is for this reason that the term "spirit guide" is an inappropriate term to describe these individuals. The only "spirit guide" we should strive to know is our own soul.

In addition, it is important to understand that invisible friends do not come into our life in order to entertain us or fulfill our fantasies (especially romantic fantasies). These people will not deceive us, but *we might easily deceive ourself* if we forget their true nature. It is very easy for wishful thinkers to plug into the fantasy department of the subconscious and invent all kinds of stories about invisible people to suit their tabloid consciousness. The key to protecting ourself against this kind of self-deception is to make sure that we are seeking truth and genuine support, not fantasies and delusions.

In this regard, it is helpful not to get caught up in trivial but exciting details about our invisible friends. It is perfectly all right to register a few quick impressions about them to give us a sense of personality, but we should not try to pick their minds for elaborate descriptions of earlier lives and intrigues—or anything that would expose us to fantasy. Such questioning is just an open invitation to our own subconscious to put on a mask and play games.

As always, the best protection against self-deception lies in invoking our highest good—becoming the right person, doing the right thing—before we attempt to strike a rapport with our invisible friends.

The following exercise is a powerful way to become more aware of the helpful presence of our invisible friends. It can be repeated as often as necessary until a good rapport is established:

We should begin with a strong aspiration to truth and the best within us. This dedication will help make sure that we focus on our mature needs for help and support, instead of activating our latent fantasies.

Then, we speculate about a key decision or issue in our own life. Are there ways of looking at these conditions we have not considered before? Are there higher perspectives to consider? What is our real need?

Have we understood fully the issues that are involved? What factors have we overlooked?

As we ponder on this decision or issue in this way, we can imagine having a conversation about it with a wise and dear friend of ours. An image of this friend may even form in our mind's eye and seem to speak to us, but it is not necessary. The important thing is that new ideas and perspectives are coming into our mind as we think.

The communication we will experience with our invisible friend will occur in whatever language we regularly use to think. Some people think in terms of words; others think in terms of images or symbols or even voices. Invisible friends speak to us by prompting ideas within our own mind, in a form that we are familiar with.

As ideas begin to pour into our awareness, we can make the communication even more effective by asking questions and pausing for answers. In this way, we soon find ourself engaged in a brainstorming session with an invisible friend!

11.

Good Psychic Manners

Wise people realize that good manners and ethics are important in interacting with other people, whether in the family, on the job, or in the community. Some of the customs of etiquette may be foolish, but we honor most of them out of respect for the people around us. The observance of ethics is a more serious issue. We act ethically in part as a gesture of goodwill toward others, but mostly because we are committed to inner values and the principles of spirit. It would be unthinkable to violate any of these standards consciously.

Obviously, not everyone honors ethical standards equally. Some people seem to have no conscience at all, and will lie, scheme, and cheat for as long as they do not get caught. Others are highly responsive to their ethics, and always act in accord with them, regardless of the circumstance. Most people, of course, fall somewhere in between.

Some people suggest that the ultimate test of ethical responsibility is simple. At times when we know that we cannot be caught, how do we act when given a chance to cheat, steal, or lie? Do we respect our inner guidelines? Or do we succumb to temptation and violate our principles for a selfish gain?

Only the immature person will succumb, of course—the person who believes himself immune to the law of cause and effect. The wise person knows that any selfish, unethical act will sooner or later generate an unpleasant consequence that must be endured. People who lie and scheme, for example, may seem to "get away with it" for years and years. In reality, however, they are only laying the foundation of a massive trap that will eventually ensnare them in circumstances even they cannot avoid. The law of cause and effect guarantees that sooner or later, these individuals will learn—from the experiences they create—that lying and cheating do not lead to prosperity. They lead instead to embarrassment, loss, and retribution.

A strong commitment to acting responsibly is an important prerequisite for leading a spiritual life. It is doubly important as our pursuit of the spiritual life leads us into the exploration of the psychic dimensions of life. Even minor psychic skills give us a tremendous advantage over people with no intuitive awareness at all—the vast majority of the physical population.

One of the first things many budding psychics discover, for example, is that they have some ability to help others with their problems. It can be very tempting to overestimate this ability and declare themselves to be a "psychic advisor." As unsuspecting people come for help, however, they may be subjected to destructive, harmful forces rather than the helpful insights that have been promised. Perhaps the untrained psychic has just had an argument with a friend. What energies is he likely to be working with? The wisdom of the spiritual plane? Or the grungy anger and malice of his own energy fields?

The ability to discern intuitively the problems and character of other people could be used constructively to help them grow and develop. But the very same information could also be used quite destructively—for example, to manipulate the trust and exploit the weaknesses of these people.

Such transgressions are highly tempting to novice psychics, because their ego blinds them to their own limitations. They are apt to believe that "no one is looking"—they are invisible and cannot be caught. But they are invisible only to the physical plane. Every action they take at psychic levels is perfectly visible to higher intelligence—and leaves a long-lasting trail by which their actions can be identified. This "trail" is what generates future circumstances and opportunities for them—under the operation of the law of cause and effect. If it is noble and helpful, they bless themselves. If it is deceitful and selfish, they damn themselves.

As we work psychically, every thought and feeling we

project stirs up the mental, astral, or etheric energies we are seeking to impress, just as a pebble, dropped in a pond, causes the water to ripple outward. We cannot afford to let any of these projections be selfish or destructive—the price we pay is just too high. It is for this reason that we must take good psychic manners seriously—and seek to uphold our psychic ethics at every juncture.

Only the person who arrogantly assumes that he is exempt from this law would knowingly abuse psychic skills and energies. Any ethical lapse, even a minor one, will lead to difficulty. Repeated lapses will lead eventually to revocation of psychic privileges—until greater responsibility is learned.

Let us therefore examine the varieties of psychic abuse—and what it means to cultivate a higher, more noble use of our psychic skills.

One of the greatest temptations to the beginning psychic is to use his or her expanded awareness to snoop and pry on others. We all have a natural curiosity about how things work. The right use of this inquisitiveness is to discover and penetrate ideas and patterns which are not apparent to others.

We must take care, however, not to let this inquisitiveness become overheated and degenerate into an excessive interest in the private lives of others. The invasion of another person's privacy is even more unethical at psychic levels than it is on the physical plane.

Psychics must therefore make sure that they are

always guided by principles of right conduct—integrity, fairness, respect for the privacy of others, and helpfulness. If their explorations lead them into an examination of the character and thoughts of others, they should ask permission beforehand of the higher selves of the people involved, and they should proceed with respect and restraint. If at any time the higher self of the other person asks the psychic to cease, the request should be honored immediately.

Without this level of restraint, psychic snooping and prying will drag us down into pettiness and sensationalism. Our minds will begin to turn into the kind of cesspool that can be found on television gossip shows—all titillation, no substance. This corrupts the fineness of our psychic sensitivity and condemns us to a very crude level of experience.

In addition, if we should happen to stick our psychic fingers into something truly rotten and devious, we may suddenly end up with a colossal headache—or find that one of our psychic fingers is missing! Indeed, too much attention to this kind of snooping can permanently orient us toward the most seamy elements of life. This will pollute our mind and create many new and unnecessary problems for us to confront in our personal life.

Another widespread problem among naïve psychics is the temptation to manipulate others. There are four common ways this urge is expressed:

1. Enticement. By beguiling or charming others

into "buying" something they do not need—such as the psychic's services or things he sells.

2. Indoctrination and exploitation. By controlling or coercing others into embracing specific beliefs or choices, as determined by the psychic.

3. Intimidation. By punishing others for their actions or inactions—through the overt expression of anger or criticism, or more indirectly, by withholding favors or support.

4. Pandering. By telling people what they want to hear, thereby exciting and strengthening their wish life—instead of helping them.

Of course, it is not just psychics who are guilty of these ethical lapses—ordinary people harbor anger, fear, and bigotry and regularly project it onto others. These projections are psychic events, and highly destructive. But as bad as it is for ordinary people to behave in this way, it is much worse for the psychic. For one thing, the psychic is learning to work with greater power, so the impact of such projections can be far more devastating. But the primary trouble is that such behavior in a psychic represents the wilful abuse of subtle energies. It calls into question the serious issue of whether the individual should be allowed to continue to operate psychically.

In its most sophisticated form, this kind of mischief may seem charming, even charismatic. The psychic may develop the ability to draw followers to him or her who will willingly suspend their own ethics, too. Once this connection is made, it is very hard to disengage from it, because our own attitudes and values quickly become warped to match the psychic's demands.

When manipulation of others is negative, it becomes a classic example of psychic attack. Instead of feeling charmed because we are "doing our master's business," we feel defeated and worthless, overwhelmed by life. Our self-esteem, judgments, and attitudes become corrupted, and we wallow in inertia. We start asking ourself, "What is the use?"

The discouraging part of this kind of attack is the discovery that the original attack by the unethical psychic probably did not cause all this mischief. We may find instead that the psychic plucked our insecurities like the strings of a harp—in other words, planted the seed of defeat in our subconscious—and then let us do all the dirty work of self-sabotage on our own!

Nonetheless, the price that is paid by the unethical psychic for any of these kinds of manipulation is extreme. If the manipulation of others becomes habitual, it will sever any real connection with the higher self for the rest of the lifetime. Genuine intuitive powers will be withdrawn, although some of the lower psychic skills may remain. Then, like a moth, the psychic will be drawn to the flame of someone even more unscrupulous than he or she.

The result is foretold by the experience of the moth.

A third variety of psychic mischief is theft—the unethical psychic may steal ideas or energies, or both.

The typical psychic thief is petty-minded—self-absorbed, egotistical, and demanding. He believes that the world owes him a break or two, and he rationalizes that it is permissable to take whatever he wants from others, rather than earn it.

Instead of learning to draw energy from the ocean of life, the psychic thief develops the very unsanitary habit of locking onto the emotional and etheric energy of those around him, and sucking them dry. Victims of this kind of psychic theft are likely to experience sudden and unjustified fatigue, confusion, and a vague sense of having been touched by something unclean.

Just as is true on the physical plane, any kind of stealing at psychic levels is forbidden. We do not have to steal to take care of ourselves under any circumstances. Psychic perception should open us up to the discovery that all of the energies of life are infinite; there is plenty for everyone, including ourself. The gulf between the haves and have nots is just an illusion of the physical plane; in reality, we are all "haves," unless we deny our connection with spirit.

The thief—whether psychic or physical—is therefore doing nothing but stealing from himself. He is denying himself the one great treasure of life—closer contact with spirit—for the silliest of gains.

The final category of psychic malfeasance could simply be called "poor psychic hygiene." Just as it would be a breach of good manners to show up in public without having bathed or changed clothes for a couple of weeks, it is a horrendous breach of psychic etiquette to project our immaturity, uncontrolled desires, petty grievances, and paranoia. It offends others—and it offends the soul.

These conditions do not necessarily take advantage of anyone else or life—but they do most definitely repel virtually every being of sensitivity. These problems of poor psychic hygiene cover a vast range, from an excessive sense of self-importance to intense criticism of the imperfections of life. Some of the most noxious are:

• Petty irritabilty—especially the childish demands and impatience of the "inner brat."

• Overheated ego and libido. Strong sexual urges are common, but just as common are projections of great personal talent and power—or advanced states of spirituality.

• The victim consciousness, where any sense of personal responsibility is denied in favor of blaming and sulking.

• Paranoia, the belief that there is a plot to destroy the quality of one's life—or, on a larger scale, a plot to destroy the overall quality of life. Examples of this problem on a world scale would be environmental extremists and anti-technology activists.

In any instance where we are controlled by a strong frustration or passion, whatever it is, we can be fairly sure we are exuding unpleasant psychic energies. We need a remedial course in psychic housecleaning to repair the damage we have done.

How do we overcome these deficiencies in psychic

ethics and etiquette? The answer is straightforward: we need to build our standards of conduct based on the laws of right human relationships, and then make sure we live up to these standards as consistently as possible. If we approach this issue casually, by masking our obnoxious behavior rather than transforming it, we will condemn ourself to endless years of suffering.

Any such code of ethics must be based on a) a deep-seated respect for the individuality of others, warts and all; and b) an equally deep love for the spirit within all of us. We do not have to invent ethics—they are spelled out for us by God in the laws that govern the universe. It is our task to understand and implement them in life.

Our concern about ethics, however, should not discourage us from exploring the psychic realms. Our spiritual design prompts us to expand our awareness and investigate the psychic worlds. We just need to be guided by common sense and the wisdom of the soul. To reject this exploration would itself be an ethical lapse.

Therefore, we need to examine how we can help other people without being intrusive. Can we support their growth without interfering with their learning process? Can we share in the lives and activities of others without denying them their individuality?

In essence, the heart of ethics is to strive to be the best person we can be at any moment in time—and to help others do the same. If we can master this simple idea, the rest of the process will fall into place.

A good base for ethical psychic activity is, of course,

a strong set of ethical standards for the way we treat other people in physical life—especially in complex situations. Almost anyone on the spiritual path knows the importance of honesty and fairness. The challenge to us lies in how we apply these principles in real life.

Perhaps we are dining in a restaurant and we see a mother yelling at her kids. We may be tempted to approach the mother and tell her how to raise her children. But would it be ethical to do so? Do we know all of the facts? They may have a history of "playing to a crowd"—embarrassing their mother in front of other people. Do we have a right to voice our opinion—or would we be imposing our beliefs and standards upon her? Would we be assuming a responsibility that is not ours to assume—or would we be acting on behalf of "the children"? How would the higher self have us act?

It is by reviewing from all angles dynamic situations such as this that we slowly learn to apply ethics in the physical plane. To extend this set of ethics to psychic work, we must likewise review potential opportunities for abuse at psychic levels. Our goal is to decide how we can best behave ethically.

Some examples to work on might include:

• What is the psychic impact of criticism on others?

• How much are we drawn to gossip and to the dark side of others? Does this extend to levels of psychic snooping?

• In what ways do we make demands of others? Do we also manipulate people at psychic levels—through the imagination, the assessment of blame, or even our wishes and hopes?

• Do we respect the achievements of our friends and colleagues, or are we envious of them? Do we support their efforts, or try to block them? What are we doing at psychic levels to project envy—or to sabotage their achievements?

• Do we tell other people how to live their lives? Are we more interested in criticizing their mistakes than in correcting ours?

12.

Recognizing Our Psychic Limitations

As we develop psychically, we gradually discover the need for precise discernment. It is all too easy to "jump to conclusions" psychically after perceiving only a few fragments of insight. Such careless perceptions, however, will lead us astray—or even worse, into nonsense.

It must also be recognized that almost every impulse reaching our awareness has been colored or conditioned by extraneous factors or forces. Unless we are able to account for these conditioning influences, and discount them in our assessments, our psychic perceptions will go awry.

Many of these conditioning factors lurk in our own subconscious, as has been described in earlier lessons—self-centered habits, a strong wish life, or rigid prejudices or stereotypes. Even a strong sense of personal inadequacy can quickly warp the quality and meaning of any psychic message we may be able to receive. Precise psychic discernment becomes possible only as we make substantial progress in cleaning up and organizing our subconscious, to eliminate these personalized patterns.

Another strong source of psychic conditioning can be found in the habits and traditions of the family in which we were raised. A constant exposure to fundamentalist Christian teachings for twenty years, for example, would make it extremely difficult for a psychic to come to terms with his or her own burgeoning abilities—let alone accept inner guidance about reincarnation, the loving nature of God, and the true meaning of life after death. We would have to make a concerted effort to "outgrow" these early instructions.

We have also examined in some depth the impact of deliberate psychic interference on our perceptions, and how such intrusions magnify our personal resentments, impatience, sadness, or even guilt, thereby crippling our ability to understand what is actually occurring.

In addition to all of these factors, there are two other, even more subtle, sources of subliminal influence that the developing psychic must learn to neutralize, lest they confuse us and distort the meanings of our psychic perceptions. The first is our cultural conditioning—the ethnic, national, and religious heritage which shapes so much of our character and thinking. The second is the conditioning power of group minds with which we are associated—a professional group, political groups, and even our generation. Even the fact that we are becoming "psychic" aligns us with an invisible group that could have a powerful influence over our thinking—and our ability to perceive life.

To perfect our psychic skills, we must learn to recognize the subtle influence of these conditioning forces in our own life—and then take steps to detach ourself from the qualities of thought and expectation that they seek to impose. We will focus on the recognition of these conditioning factors in this lesson, and take up the topic of disentangling ourself from them in the next chapter.

The impact of cultural conditioning can be seen most clearly as we visit foreign countries and interact with the people living there. These are decent people, much like ourselves, but with distinct customs—some of which strike us as peculiar, perhaps even repulsive. These customs, in turn, are the result of the different values, habits, and traditions that embody this country's culture generation after generation.

Every one is subtly influenced by national values and traditions at unconscious levels. In Japan, for example, it was long accepted that the noblest act to take after bringing great shame or defeat upon family or country was suicide. Yet in other countries, the act of suicide under any circumstances brings shame and humiliation upon the surviving family!

The impact of this cultural conditioning is largely beneficial. It helps to socialize the youth in any society, so that they learn to fit in with their peer group and the culture as a whole. Nonetheless, as our attention turns more and more to discovering the light of spirit, we must develop the ability to see beyond these limits and embrace the inner realities of divine life.

Cultural conditioning is not just limited to national traditions, however. Even stronger cultural factors influencing us can be our clan or ethnic ties, our religion, and our gender.

The whole tradition of passing money, position, and prerogative on to the next generation through inheritance is an example of the importance of the clan, even in our modern society. The right to pass position and wealth on to an heir is one of the most fundamental precepts of English common law. It suggests—and enforces—the notion that unless we are a child of someone of importance, we cannot play an important role in society. Fortunately, the omnipotence of this precept is beginning to crumble. But most of us make important decisions throughout life based on this principle, without ever understanding how we are influenced by it!

Ethnic conditioning affects us in much the same way. One ethnic group may prize genius and individual effort; the legacy of another ethnic group may discourage its members from doing anything that would set them apart from the rest of their group. If people from these two ethnic backgrounds try to work together, their differing cultural values regarding work will inevitably clash.

The patterns of cultural conditioning are often easiest to discern in terms of religious teachings and traditions. A lifetime of believing that everyone who does not believe as we do is going to suffer eternally in hell dramatically affects the way in which we interact with anyone we believe fits that description. It becomes virtually impossible, for example, to live up to Christ's injunction to love our neighbor as ourself. Our religious stereotypes have robbed us of the ability to respect our neighbor, who is surely going to hell.

Even the cultural assumptions that go with being male or female affect us in these ways—and the impact has become far more dramatic than ever during the last fifty years. We are told that men are from Mars and women are from Venus, or some other similar nonsense, and then strive mightily to live up to whatever these roles imply. In truth, we are human beings who have often been male as well as female in past lives. We are meant to blend together both male and female characteristics, just as God does. The effort to be either a macho male or a feisty female will lead us into much silliness.

It is important to understand that these traditions and attitudes are *primarily* conveyed to us at unconscious levels, psychically. We are given verbal hints, to be sure, but the real message is conveyed subliminally, through our personal connections to these cultural units. It is for this reason that a psychic is vulnerable to serious distortion and confusion until he or she learns to disable these connections long enough to make an objective perception.

In tuning into a man-hating feminist, for example,

the average psychic is simply apt to let the client's strong anti-male prejudices influence his or her perceptions. A more developed psychic, on the other hand, who has learned not to be fooled by automatic cultural conditioning, would be able to discern that the client's problems do not originate with men, but with her own rebelliousness and rejection of authority. The client is using gender conditioning as a shield to hide her immaturity.

The second great category of subliminal conditioning we must prepare ourselves to handle is the impact of group minds connected with us. Our cultural conditioning begins when we are an infant and lasts throughout our whole life—or until we learn to see it for what it is. Most of the links we have with group minds, by contrast, have been made since we became an adult. They include:

- Work or professional groups. The healing profession has a strong group mind, as does the legal profession, engineers, and accountants. Public school teachers have a distinct group mind, college professors a different one.
- An ideological group. Political conservatives form one group mind, political liberals a distinctly different one. People who are envious of the achievements of the wealthy form a group mind that feeds their jealousy and discontent. People who love poetry or fine art form a group mind. People who believe in God's benevolence form a group that supersedes traditional religious lines.

• Support groups. Recovering alcoholics form a group mind which is highly important in their recovery process.

• Generations. The central mood of each generation influences everything from tastes in music and style to values, priorities, and expectations.

• Social activists. The willingness of the public to accept sweeping changes in our cultural assumptions without significant thought or discussion indicates how powerfully we can be affected at unconscious levels. What turned a nation of smokers into a nation that persecutes smokers within twenty years? A powerful influence. What turned a nation that idolized "independent cusses" into a society of robotic recyclers? If we were suddenly liberated from the spoken and unspoken propaganda of social activists, how would we think about these issues?

• Groups of malcontents. There are many people who look at life and dwell on its warts, rather than its opportunities. These people become alienated from the evolutionary impulses of humanity—and try to take others with them. They deliberately use fear to raise money, promote pessimism, and short-circuit reason. An occasional moment of alienation can attract us to these groups, which will then stimulate deep veins of discontent within our own feeling. As a result, we end up feeling alienated from God, who gets blamed for the entire self-inflicted mess.

These group minds differ from cultural conditioners in several key ways. First, they are more highly focused and organized. They have goals to reach, an agenda to fulfill. We will be used to achieve those goals and implement the agenda. Second, there is a greater demand for loyalty. It is assumed that most Americans will remain American citizens. A group of social activists, on the other hand, recognizes that our tie to the group is far more tenuous. So they demand conspicuous acts of loyalty—and treat us harshly if we stray from the common dogma. We are seldom allowed to think for ourself. Thinking is a sign of weakening commitment.

Our sense of identity is likewise tampered with. It is not enough to be an American first, a Methodist second, and a lawyer third. We must demonstrate that we are a True Believer first—be that a gay, a minority, a woman, or whatever—and everything else second. Our cause becomes the central structure of our life—and our sense of who we are.

In both instances, however, these strong conditioning forces exert tremendous pressure on the thinking and behavior of each human member. Since developing psychics are trying to become more consciously receptive to unconscious impulses and influences, the potential impact upon such an individual is even greater—until we learn to deal with these pressures effectively. These pressures can subtly skew the focus of attention of the psychic, his or her attitude toward the topic being investigated, and his or her interpretation of what is perceived.

The disruption of the focus of attention is best illustrated by the tendency of naïve psychics to tune into leftover emotional thoughtforms of spiritual figures (such as Mary or the Christ) and mistake them for the genuine spiritual presence. A similar phenomenon would be the tendency of many Tarot "readers" to tune into the gypsy fortune-telling thoughtforms surrounding the Tarot, rather than the real powers.

The attitudes of many psychics today are subtly influenced by popular ideas of sociological or political thinking. A psychic might be heavily conditioned by our societal fear of death and dying, for example, and be completely unable to help specific individuals see that their terminal illnesses are in fact the healing they seek. Their corrupted attitude makes it impossible to read the situation correctly.

The failure to interpret impressions correctly as a result of unconscious conditioning can be seen in the tendency of many psychics to warn of dangers that lie ahead without recognizing the opportunity for growth, discovery, and creativity within these situations. The pessimism of cultural forces magnifies whatever fear still lies within the psychic's subconscious and subverts the interpretation.

It must be kept in mind that most of these cultural and group influences are beneficial for most human beings. They lift up the immature and undeveloped and help them operate at a higher standard. But it is absolutely crucial that we maintain a high sense of individual responsibility, or these influences can easily turn dangerous and vicious. The attractiveness of either terrorism on an international scale or gang violence on an individual scale is their seeming ability to give powerless people a tremendous advantage over others. It is justified by the "us versus them" mentality of many groups.

These influences are able to condition any one of us to whatever degree we draw strength, power, and authority from our participation in these groups, rather than from God. If we draw our sense of identity and self-importance from being a feminist, a Native American, or part of the Establishment, we are building a strong connection that allows our chosen group to manipulate us, both directly and indirectly. In addition, we begin to shape our expectations based on this unconscious conditioning, rather than on independent observation of life.

Some of this conditioning, of course, is direct—based on following the example of role models set before us. But every belief, habit, and value that we have as a human being is accompanied by a psychic equivalent—a strong force that exists at unconscious levels. These psychic equivalents can be played upon and conditioned directly at unconscious levels, through the contacts we have with groups and cultural associations. The group itself serves as a huge psychic battery charged by the traditions and beliefs of many generations. The stronger our bond with any group is, the more we become enslaved to domination and manipulation by our association with it.

How do we break this connection? The answer is simple. We must start thinking for ourself.

We must recognize that we do not need to rely on the stereotypes and prejudices of these groups to make our way in life. Deep within us, in the light of the soul, we are able to see clearly on any issue of life. Our primary connection should always be to this higher self, the seat of our higher intelligence. All other connections must be subordinate to it.

It is therefore indispensable to the work of developing psychic awareness to learn to recognize how we have been subtly influenced by cultural conditioning and the limitations of group minds—not for the purpose of rejecting it, but for the purpose of disentangling ourselves from its web of confusion. Only once we have some awareness of our true connection with spirit does it become absolutely clear how limiting our previous connections have been.

The work of learning to think for ourself begins by reflecting on how we have previously thought about certain key issues—and then comparing it to how the highest intelligence within us views these same issues. Numerous issues can be reviewed in this way:

- What is our attitude toward the work ethic?
- How do we usually view triumphs—and tragedies?
- What is our view toward the opposite sex?
- What is the extent of our power to influence or shape the events of life?
- What is the basis of our identity?
- What is the nature of our connection with divinity—or with our ethnic heritage?

There are, of course, many other similar questions that could be posed.

As we work with any one of these questions, it is also important to inquire:

1. What has been our attitude toward this issue? What do we value in this regard?

2. What are the roots of this belief—when did we first adopt it? Were we inspired by the higher self—or did we just accept someone else's opinion?

3. Has this attitude been helpful—or harmful?

4. What attitude or expectation would best serve our highest good at the present time?

5. How should our belief or value be updated?

By completing these reviews, we will learn to discern the influences of these conditioning forces in our life—and set the stage so that we can learn to reverse the conditioning process.

13.

Transcending Psychic Limitations

It is not enough to understand that we, as agents of light, are limited by sundry cultural, ethnic, and collective attitudes and influences—and that these subtle pressures may be very powerful in preventing us from looking upon the key issues of life as the soul views them. Having penetrated the miasma of misapprehension in mass consciousness, as we did in the last lesson, we must take the challenge of these limiting forces one step further:

We must learn to rise above them in our thinking.

In other words, we must learn to think for ourself, inspired directly by the wisdom of the light within us. We must not spurn conventional truths simply because they are conventional; this would be simple rebelliousness. But we must train ourself to penetrate through all of the beliefs, assumptions, and values that society accepts without even a momentary reflection. We must orient ourself to the intelligence of the soul, so that we will not accept anything less than the real.

H.G. Wells dealt with this problem directly in one of his lesser-known novels, *In The Days of the Comet.* Writing in the first decade of the century, he spins a story told some 60 or 70 years later, looking backwards to a society that is completely trapped in its beliefs, customs, and assumptions. He writes with particular force in describing the schemes that were being set forth to solve the problems of the day—schemes such as socialism and communism. He suggests that until the basic problems of human unkindness and ignorance are solved, such massive reform movements will inevitably make society's problems worse, not better.

A strange comet approaches earth, ignored by all except the most visionary scientists. The tail of the comet brushes the earth's atmosphere just as war in Europe breaks out—a war that is strikingly similar to World War I. But as a mysterious green element in the comet's tail touches our atmosphere, all humans throughout the world lose consciousness for an hour or two.

As they awaken, at daybreak, they have a new level of understanding. They have not been made perfect beings, but warfare and personal malice now seem pointless. They understand the value of cooperation, and treat one another with respect. Having undergone The Great Change, they set about remaking human society in a more enlightened fashion.

Through the stark contrast between the actual conditions of the early 20th century and the ideal conditions that result from the comet, Wells is able to show how totally we succumb to the pressures of conventional wisdom and popular thought. Even our "solutions" tend to be colored by the problems themselves far more than by the potential to resolve them.

In this way, Wells brilliantly points out the need for clear thinking, inspired by the soul rather than cultural or ethnic prejudices and traditions. He does not create an Utopia, where no one can do wrong, for that would be impossible. Instead, he creates a society which underscores the importance of knowing who we are—and thinking for ourselves.

In our personal lives, this great change occurs as we make the effort to rise above cultural, national, and racial assumptions—not by rejecting or fighting against these perspectives, but by understanding that there are alternatives to them. As we open our minds to this higher level of comprehension, it becomes possible for the comet of our own higher intelligence to sweep through our individual values, priorities, assumptions, and tenets, discarding the ones that limit us and replacing them with a bold new understanding of reality.

This change represents the first great step toward creating a truly open mind.

The first step is the most difficult. We must admit to ourself that we have been unduly influenced—perhaps even duped—by the "party line" beliefs and principles of some group, culture, race, or religion. This step is troublesome because most intelligent people firmly believe that they are, indeed, open-minded. They have little awareness of how much their thinking has been shaped by the dominant forces of their upbringing and environment.

The ardent feminist, for example, has very little awareness of how rigidly her thinking is controlled by feminist dogma, even when it contradicts common sense.

The militant fundamentalist is equally ignorant of how limited his or her intellectual inquiry into the nature of life has been—and how much of it has been dictated by the creeds and thoughts of unknown theologians.

The typical survivor of the Holocaust—any holocaust—has no idea how much his or her world view is saturated by the sense of victimhood.

The average college-educated person has scant awareness of how little he or she knows about death and the ongoing nature of life, and how much his or her emotional and mental stability depends upon the denial of his or her profound ignorance.

Even most spiritual aspirants have only an inkling of how often their aspirations lead to nonsense and silliness, rather than to enlightenment. Instead of seeking out the light of the soul, they allow themselves to be drawn toward whatever happens to be popular—or at least the latest craze. They prefer the approval of others over the discovery of truth and light.

It is not easy to admit to ourself that we have been

unduly influenced by the causes we believe in—or even by our cultural background and connections. But this, nevertheless, is where we must begin. We must ask:

• What are the major groups we are aligned with, by choice or by life circumstance? A political party would be a group we align with by choice. An ethnic tie would link us to our ethnic heritage by life circumstance.

• Have we ever thought through and examined why we are guided by the principles and customs of this group? Or are we in any way terrified of even questioning these assumptions? If yes, then why? Are we loyal to the group because we respect its values and authority—or are we just afraid of rejection?

• How do we know that the beliefs and programs of this group are valid? Have we tested them in our own life? Do they make sense to us? Or are they based on wild assumptions and conclusions requiring great leaps of faith?

• What would be the end result of implementing the programs and proposals of this group? If we accept the notion, for example, that government is responsible for providing for the welfare of its citizens, what would be the end result of implementing this concept? Is it possible? Is it feasible? What kind of society would result?

• Do the acts of the group match their stated motives and principles? If a spiritual group spends most of its time spreading fear and anxiety, how can it be spiritual? Fear and anxiety are not spiritual qualities. If a group that claims to promote peace and cooperation actually spreads hatred and alienation, how can it be viewed as an agent of peace?

• Does the group welcome inquiry and questioning from its members, or does it stifle dissension? If you choose to leave the group, does it harass you—or let you leave in good grace?

• Does participation in the group actually create obstacles that make our future growth more difficult? If a group actively teaches its members that there is no inner life, then it is making the future growth of its members far more difficult than it need be. If a group belittles its members and tells them that they derive all of their self-worth—or hope for salvation—by belonging to this group, then it is constructing huge barriers that will have to be hurdled in the future.

If we find, through this examination, that any one or more of the groups in our life do dominate our thinking, deliberately or accidentally, we must resolve to detach ourself. This does not necessarily mean dropping out of the group. It would be impossible, after all, to drop out of our ethnic heritage, our generation, or our gender! But we can detach from the conditioning influences of habitual perspectives. We can resolve to start thinking for ourself.

The process of learning to think for ourself begins by taking charge of our individuality. As the Delphic oracle told the ancient Greeks: "Know Thyself." Shakespeare embellished this admonition, adding: "and to thine own self be true." We must take this advice to heart and examine who we truly are. Are we an American? A Catholic, Jew, Moslem, Protestant, or agnostic? A man or a woman? A liberal or a conservative? A have or a have not? Or a human being?

Making this determination is important, because we tend to draw great strength from our sense of identity. Victims often draw their identities from the horrible events they have suffered, be it child abuse or a Holocaust. For them, the events they have endured severely limit their understanding of life. The egomaniac, on the other hand, tends to draw his or her identity from the defeat of other people, which restricts the capacity to interact harmoniously with others. Most of us draw our sense of identity from our "blood lines"—from our ancestors, our ethnic ties, and the customs of our home land. These genealogical ties can be quite strong, as demonstrated by the Americans of Chinese descent who have been pressured on the basis of their ethnic background to spy on behalf of Red China.

To break these ties, we must begin to view ourself first and foremost as an agent of light—a child of God with a birthright of spiritual strengths, qualities, and talents. No tie on the physical planes can ever justify betraying this inner spiritual reality. In this way, we gradually come to see ourself as an agent of light first, and an American second; a human being first, and a man or a woman second; a child of God first, and a Jew or a Christian or a Hindu second. We establish a proper priority in our sense of identity.

Once we have a proper sense of who we are, the

next step is to answer a series of questions concerning how we intend to act in life. These questions include:

What do we stand for? Have we "bought" into limited programs and attitudes that dictate our thinking day by day? Or do we have a coherent, well-defined set of values and principles that shape our thinking, no matter what events may arise?

In this country, for example, "freedom" is a buzzword that is used by both the left and the right to justify whatever programs they advance. As a result, it is often used to gain support for proposals that will actually deprive the public of its freedoms. This can only happen in a climate where people have not thought through what freedom is and what it means to preserve it. Freedom has become a platitude, rather than a principle. We may be willing to die for it, but we do not even bother to define—for ourself—what it means!

If we wish to become an intelligent citizen, therefore, we ought to start by defining the meaning of freedom, and then evaluate all of our beliefs—political, religious, and personal—in terms of whether or not they promote freedom or undermine it. And we should do the same for other key ideas, values, and priorities that guide our life.

What kind of lifestyle best expresses our inner self? This stage of self-examination should begin with a careful review of our goals. What are we trying to accomplish? Will these goals serve the interests of the soul? Once we understand our goals, then we can evaluate what kind of lifestyle is best suited to achieving them. Do we need to be in the forefront of social change, or would it be better to work quietly behind the scenes? Do we need to lead a crusade for reform, or would it be more effective to set a good example as an enlightened parent, employee, or citizen? Do we need to be passive and negative—or should we be active and aggressive?

Contrary to public opinion, these are choices each of us make, consciously or otherwise. A childhood of abuse does not drive anyone to become a loud-mouthed victim as an adult; quite the contrary, the adult makes a deliberate decision to make a career out of being a victim. Such adults trap themselves in a lifestyle that impoverishes them and betrays their higher purposes.

Just so, a childhood of poverty does not consign anyone to the junk heap of the homeless. Once we are an adult, life tends to give us thousands of opportunities to defeat poverty and become self-reliant. If we fail to seize these opportunities, it is our own fault. We have let our sense of poverty entrap us, instead of harnessing the best within us.

What are our priorities? The average person never thinks about values, ethics, and priorities, unless forced to do so by unpleasant events. In those conditions, however, no real thinking occurs, because the effort to think becomes obscured by uncontrolled emotional responses to the crisis. It is therefore important to think through our values and priorities in advance of crisis, when we can be reasonably objective and detached from popular convention.

In making this evaluation, we must be aware of

how much our thinking tends to be conditioned by negative values—our personal comfort, our security, our freedom, and our good feelings. When caught between contradictory forces, most of us will opt simply for the most risk-free alternative—rather than the one that may bring the most life of spirit into the situation. Succumbing to such pressures does not solve the conflict—it merely complicates it.

As much as possible, we must strive to establish values and priorities that are based on the principles of the higher self. This requires a long period of reevaluation, for while the personality thinks in terms of its own self-interest, the soul thinks in terms of the good of humanity as a whole. While the personality thinks in terms of its own comfort, the soul thinks in terms of making life more enlightened. While the personality just wants to feel good about life, the soul wants to be an agent of goodness and growth.

How do we see our world? Do we look at it through the eyes of the soul—or through the eyes of a timid, battered personality?

If we view the world and its events through the eyes of the soul, it will seem to us to be abundant, friendly, and filled with opportunity—a place where we can expand our talents, prosper, enjoy companionship, and flourish. But if we view the world and its events through the eyes of a victimized personality, we may well see it as frightening, intimidating, irrational, and dead—a place where the most we can expect is to prevent complete disaster.

The contrast in these two views is staggering—but it is the correct measurement of the difference between the enlightened and the unenlightened personality.

Once we have defined our individuality, we must then begin the lengthy process of integrating this new world view into all of our beliefs, principles, attitudes, and assumptions. This work will require nothing less than a total overhaul of our character, but the payoff is well worth the effort. In the end, we will be far more responsive to spirit than before, and largely immune to the limiting influences of cultural and group pressures on our thinking.

The actual work is easy enough, once we grasp the basic concept. We take a specific idea or belief that we have embraced as part of our understanding of life. We then ask ourself: what is the origin of this belief? When did I first embrace it as a thought of my own? What was my source? Did I carefully evaluate it at the time—or did it just appeal to me emotionally? Has it helped me or limited me? Is this my own thinking—or someone else's?

At this stage, we should then try to look at this issue from the perspective of the soul, our highest intelligence. What is the highest perspective? What belief would best serve divine goodwill or justice or joy? As much as possible, we should try to appeal to our spiritual intuition to guide and illumine us on the larger issues involved. Depending upon our intuitive skills, it may take many repeated efforts to come to a full understanding of the issue at hand. But if we stick with it, our effort will be rewarded.

Once we have gained this insight, we must then reshape our thinking to accommodate it—not just on this one issue, but in every way that we have reacted to or compensated for this issue in our life.

Perhaps we attended a college where we became enchanted by the Marxist philosophy of life. Later, as we learn about the failure of the communist economic system and the genocide practiced by communist regimes, we begin to question our commitment to this belief. Employing this method, we would ask ourself: why was I first attracted to this ideology? From whom did I learn about Marxism? Did they give me facts—or propaganda? Has it helped me or hurt me? How does the soul view this issue? What is the impact of Marxism on human individuality? Does it promote growth—or stunt it?

Once this review is completed, a new view of social compassion will begin to emerge—a more enlightened view. We would then need to take this new perspective and use it to update every belief and attitude that we formed during the decade in which we were enthralled by Marxism—even hard-to-detect unconscious responses. Only once the outdated belief in Marxism is thoroughly cleansed from our consciousness can we consider the process complete.

This work is a slowly evolving process—the work of our entire lifetime. We recognize the stereotypes that have conditioned us one by one, then think through new values and priorities that would serve us better.

But there is a good reason why this work must be slow and deliberate. The psychic force from which each stereotype and limited belief is formed tends to magnify its power in our own perception. This is because these thoughtforms have roots in a nearly-infinite pool of psychic energy. In the case of Marxism, for example, the pool of psychic energy has been sustained by millions of people world wide. It is no simple matter to pull up our own personal roots and be done with it. Once we have, in fact, we will be apt to experience repercussions. Our change of mind will leave us troubled and oddly disconnected. We will taste a sense of disapproval, and wonder if we are on the right track. We may even be confronted physically by people who will accuse us of betraying the commitments we have made.

Do not discount the power of this pressure: in many cases, it is the mainstream of our heritage. If we are a Jew or Christian or Hindu trying to detach from our cultural limitations, we will have to withstand the self-righteous disapproval of those we "leave behind"—both physically and psychically. The psychic pressure is usually far more intense than the physical—and more dangerous, because it is so subtle and persistent.

It is this undying pressure that keeps so many people immersed in tribal consciousness. They love the security and warm feelings that come from belonging to their group. Even if the group is clearly harmful, as in the case of a gang, the individual members will be reluctant to break ranks.

In order to become agents of light, however, we must

learn to belong above all to the soul, rather than temporary human groups. We must become part of the family of God, and recognize that this inner, spiritual family is far greater and more significant than our tribal or cultural family.

Indeed, these cultural and ethnic limitations are all earthbound forces. As long as our primary allegiance—our identity—is pledged to any group on earth, it will be impossible to enter fully into the light of the soul. As the agent of light develops and grows, therefore, it becomes clear that his or her cultural and ethnic ties become so much excess baggage that must be jettisoned.

The lure of the familiar and comfortable is in fact usually a handicap to our aspirations to excellence—and spirit.

The best way to develop the insight we need in order to think for ourself is to start looking at key situations in our life from the perspective of the soul. This can best be done by examining the core beliefs and values that color our thinking about life, death, politics, sex, duty, or honor.

As we examine a core value, we must begin by defining the stereotyped thinking being advanced by various conflicting "experts." How do they limit and restrict understanding, even while embodying a sliver of truth?

The second step is to determine which stereotype has tended to govern our own thinking. What impact has this had on us?

The third step is to define how the soul views this issue. What is the bigger picture which almost everyone is missing? It will be necessary to use some spiritual intuition to make these evaluations. But we must keep in mind that the soul's views will almost certainly be substantially different from what we have believed in the past.

The soul would not ask, for example, how blacks and whites differ, and what issues keep them apart. It would ask: what do all people have in common? What is the basis for building cooperation among the races, based on these common concerns? How can we emphasize the shared goals, values, and concerns of blacks, whites, and all the rest of the hues, so that humanity can learn to work together?

Finally, once we perceive the insight of the soul, we must integrate it into our personal values, ethics, and attitudes, so that we reflect and express the very best within us.

14.

Enriching Life Psychically

In paying a visit to friends, we generally expect to be welcomed in a gracious and cheerful manner. We hope the atmosphere will be cordial and pleasing. In part, it is the duty of the host and hostess to set the tone for such an uplifting environment, but as guests, we likewise bear some responsibility for creating and sustaining the proper mood. If we are grumpy or sarcastic, our gloom will poison the atmosphere and seep quickly into the reactions of others. By contrast, if we are upbeat and cheerful, we will set a far more pleasing tone—and may even neutralize the complaints or self-absorption of others. Knowing this, we willingly discipline ourself to remain polite and avoid saying anything that might upset the friendliness of our visit.

Unfortunately, we often let down our guard once we have said our "goodbyes." Thinking we are now safe to speak our mind, we can scarcely wait to start gushing forth negative comments about the people we have left, the refreshments that were offered, and the decor of the home. We believe, erroneously, that our statements and condemnations will have no effect at all, just because we are no longer in the physical company of the other people.

As we learn more about the psychic dimensions of life, however, we discover that such thoughts and comments do have an impact. Any thought or feeling about another person, helpful or harmful, immediately links us with the subconscious levels of that individual's awareness. A negative thought or critical remark may not ever be registered consciously by this person, but it is certainly known subconsciously—and instantly pollutes the quality of our relationship.

To become a responsible agent of light, we must begin to respect the inner dimensions of our life as well as the tangible, outer ones. We must extend the discipline of our polite behavior to include our comments and unspoken thoughts as well.

There is no such thing as a "private thought." The moment we give shape to a thought or a feeling, it immediately links us to any person, idea, or object related to it. A thought of blessing a sick person, for example, will link us to the infinite resources of healing power—and to the person we are focused on. In this way, we can become an effective channel for helping this individual. But the same power is more often used to harm. A feeling of bitterness or envy directed toward another person—even in our imagination alone—instantly assaults that other person at subconscious levels. Worse, it strengthens the bond that already exists between us, and draws us more closely into relationship with the very person we dislike!

Many different thoughts and feelings pour through our awareness every day. Some people just observe them, and think they can do nothing to stop or redirect them. But the budding agent of light discovers that the same kind of self-control that we use to set a tone of cordiality in the company of others can be mastered and applied to disciplining our internal awareness. We can cleanse the body of our negative thoughts and feelings—and we can learn to use thoughts to create a pleasing and cordial atmosphere in which to live psychically.

There are two steps involved in learning this lesson. The first is to stop doing harm to others, even by entertaining negative thoughts and feelings. The second is to begin using our thoughts to create a healthy, enjoyable environment—an environment that supports the efforts of others.

The choice is ours—and it is one of the most fundamental choices we make in life. After all, it will be one of the most important factors in determining the quality of our life—and our ability to enjoy it.

Every thought and feeling we entertain is composed of psychic energy. As we reflect on these thoughts or brood on these feelings, we shape them into well-defined shapes known as "thoughtforms." Since our perceptions are highly colored by our physical experiences, most of these thoughtforms are finite and earthbound. The jealous force of possessiveness, for example, might well appear in the form of a psychic leash connecting us constantly to the spouse we distrust. If our jealousy and distrust are especially intense, the leash may even end in a psychic "choke collar" around our spouse's neck.

A thoughtform is a kind of psychic battery containing a specific quantity and quality of thought or feeling. In the case of the choke collar, the thoughtform is charged with a destructive measure of jealousy and distrust, and is activated every time those feelings arise in the person's consciousness. In this way, these undisciplined feelings poison the consciousness of the thinker, attacks the consciousness of the spouse, and destabilizes the relationship itself.

Even if the distrustful person eventually divorces the spouse, the relationship will remain active through this bond of jealousy—and will continue to warp his or her interactions in other intimate relationships. It will sow fresh seeds of distrust and jealousy in every future marriage, until it is dispelled.

Attitudes of hate, gloom, and defeat likewise can give the thoughtforms we construct highly potent charges, thereby dooming our attempts to become better people even before we start trying. But the very same principle can help us as well as harm us. If we deliberately create thoughtforms filled with respect, cooperation, trust, cheerfulness, and support, they will become magnetically charged with goodwill, joy, and friendship.

These powerfully-charged thoughtforms accumulate in our subconscious, forming patterns or habits. If we spend most of our time brooding, sulking, or loathing, we will fill our aura with murky energies and frightening images. Even worse, this brooding will magnetically attract us to the things we resent or fear. On the other hand, if we spend most of our time focused in gratitude, enthusiasm, and contentment, our aura will be replete with highly energized thoughtforms that attract good friends, opportunities to succeed, and help when it is needed. In either case, it is only a matter of time before our behavior is almost entirely determined by the nature of these thoughtforms.

But it is not just our own personal aura that will be corrupted—or enriched. Even if we are making a concerted effort to be polite, our aura radiates the dominant forces captured in these thoughtforms. If we are a pessimist, we will leave behind us a swath of despair and gloom wherever we go—the office, our home, or even a friend's house. If we are worried sick about a big decision, we will likewise saturate our surroundings with anxiety.

Fortunately, there is the same opportunity to enrich our surroundings—if our character is filled with the "right stuff." If we are usually cheerful and generous, these qualities will bless our home and our office. If we carry with us faith and goodwill, we can enrich a hospital room with healing love and hope. We can likewise bless a church or temple with holiness.

Due to the nature of the psychic dimensions, it is not even necessary to visit a building or location in order to pollute—or enrich—it. If a loved one is undergoing an ordeal in a distant city, it may not be feasible to visit in person. But it is perfectly reasonable to saturate his home or office with the light and strength of goodwill. The impact will be even stronger if we clearly visualize thoughtforms that embody these forces—for example, a star filled with healing love or an embrace glowing with goodwill.

The same principle, of course, also applies to negativity. The possessive lust of a sex addict can cross thousands of miles as easily as it can cross a room. The self-absorption of a business person can alienate potential clients half a world away as easily as if they were sitting in his or her office.

When left unchecked, the psychic nature of our thoughts and feelings can quickly entrap us in the flaws of our character. The result is a loss of control in numerous areas of our life:

- We feel trapped by circumstances.
- We become stifled by our relationships.
- We seem to be estranged from our higher self.
- We have a general sense of dismay and despair.

All of these problems, of course, are self-inflicted. We are letting the psychic nature of life defeat us, rather than exercising our maturity to regain self-control. It is just as easy to use this aspect of our psychic life to enrich our environment as it is to corrupt it.

The feedback of life tells us which way we have

chosen. If we radiate gloom, the reaction of those around us will increase our gloom. If we are angry, the response of those we lash out at will deepen our ire. If we are guilty, the echoes returning to us from "out there" will intensify our sense of wrongness.

On the other hand, the constant expression of gratitude toward others will lead inexorably to new opportunities. A strong measure of enthusiasm for our work will open up a new appreciation for excellence. And a sense of closeness with our Creator will build an environment of togetherness.

Every thoughtform, astral or mental, consists of three elements or parts:

1. The image or form itself. By itself, the image is mundane, no more meaningful than a photograph. The image is just the outer appearance of the thoughtform.

2. Its significance—the link this thoughtform establishes between us and some other person, idea, or force. Properly charged, the image of a double-edged sword could link us with the power to shatter illusion and clean out negativity. But the same image could also be linked to a poor self-image and a tendency to inflict wounds upon ourself.

3. Its power. Millions of thoughtforms of Jesus have been created over the centuries by pious Christians. Almost none of them is actually connected with the presence of Jesus. As a result, they have little power other than the faint strength of their own wishes and hopes.

Most thoughtforms created by the average person to bless or enrich life are weak and ineffectual, because they are vague and held only briefly in our thoughts. They have never been properly connected with a divine link. On the other hand, most thoughtforms created of hate, jealousy, bitterness, or lust are strong and influential, because they are more intense, sustained, and specifically focused—as if they had been set in concrete and filled with power every time we re-energize our negativity.

As an agent of light, we need to recognize our responsibility to create only those thoughtforms that will enrich the earth plane. A careless fascination with the thought of catastrophe, for example, can create a psychic force that can then mislead less discerning intuitives. A distorted idea such as "original sin" can pollute the thinking of humanity for hundreds of years.

It is of little value to despair over the vast number of impure thoughtforms which contaminate human thinking and feeling like so much sludge in a sewer. Nevertheless, each of us can assure that we do not add to the cesspool that already exists. We can achieve this goal by regulating our personal thinking and feeling, and making sure that all of our thoughts and emotions elevate human thinking. In this way, we develop a capacity to enrich life psychically.

There are four simple ways to focus our thoughts and feelings to enrich life.

The most obvious is to discipline our responses to

irritating conditions. It is a fact of life that unpleasant events happen to all of us. Some can be avoided, but most cannot—an unexpected increase in our work load, an illness, rotten weather, traffic jams, and, of course, the demands of rude and obnoxious people. But even though we may not be able to avoid such conditions, we can certainly choose to respond to them with the highest and noblest elements within us—patience, dignity, wisdom, and courage.

Bitterness, impatience, fear, and depression are common but inappropriate responses to the challenges of life. They are a blight on health and happiness—both in the aura of the person expressing them and in the greater aura of mass consciousness. It is the duty of each person to learn to act with a proper measure of self-control and not succumb to these negative traps.

A second important way to use our psychic nature to enrich life is to deliberately bless significant areas of life that we have taken for granted. Blessing is the act of focusing our attention on the seed of greatness and nobility within any person or aspect of life and magnifying its connection with its divine essence. Our power to bless is unlimited; we can bless the family and friends who have supported us, the talents and opportunities that have been given to us so that we might succeed, our job or career, our health, and the spirit of democracy and the opportunity to live in a free country.

A third way to enrich life psychically is by projecting a positive, optimistic expectation about life into the future. It may seem safe to be pessimistic about our future prospects, but such negativity creates a psychic undertow that may well drag us under the incoming wave of divine possibilities. It is a very unintelligent way to approach life. It is far better to look to the future with high expectations about work, our ability to overcome an illness, the potential to enrich a relationship, or even the opportunity to transform a bad habit into something more enlightened.

On occasion, these expectations can be quite specific. In working to improve a marital relationship, for example, it can be helpful to examine the bond as it currently exists psychically—to evaluate where it needs strengthening. Then, we can create thoughtforms appropriate to the relationship that we link with love, respect, cooperation, support, and other noble qualities. The more often we build such thoughtforms and reinforce them, the more effectively we build a psychic base for a strong relationship.

The fourth simple way to enrich life psychically is to make a regular habit of expressing gratitude to our Creator for all of the blessings we have received throughout life—and for those that are yet to come. This expression of thanksgiving should include our appreciation for guidance and protection; health and healing; the opportunity to develop and use a discerning mind; a loving, generous heart; and patience and inner strength.

Through gratitude, we link our daily thoughts and feelings to the transcendental power of divine life, thus transforming our own inner life. In this fact lies the secret of adding meaning to all that we do.

In training ourself to enrich life psychically, we must assume the responsibility to consciously control our responses to life. When we would otherwise become irritated, we need to respond with poise and tolerance, rather than rudeness and complaint. When we would previously have become angry, we need to respond with forgiveness and insight. We must also realize that we cannot afford to wait until all of our problems disappear on their own; we must take steps to control our response to these conditions.

In short, we must stand ready to replace old habits with new ones. And so, we should review our typical responses to life's challenges. How, for example, do we tend to respond when others criticize us? Defensively? Angrily? With self-pity?

In responding in this way, are we enriching our aura—or polluting it? Are we ennobling morale at work—or poisoning it? Are we enriching mass consciousness—or polluting it? If we are polluting, how can we change our thinking and feeling so that we stop polluting and begin enriching?

An important part of making this review is assessing how much energy we waste in reacting to unpleasant situations we cannot control. There is nothing we can do to alter the weather, taxes, or traffic. Our only practical option is to accept the conditions that arise as gracefully as possible. But there are some situations where we can have an impact—as in parenting or improving a marital relationship. In these instances, we must restrain the temptation to complain about what is wrong and focus instead on what we can do to heal the situation.

In addition, we must inspect the inner connections we have established in this aspect of life. Do our attitudes link us to the best within us and our experiences, or to the worst—such as criticism or retribution toward others? Do we frequently draw on our storehouse of resentment, doubt, or gloom to shape our conscious feelings—or do we recognize and appreciate our strength and blessings, and rely on them in shaping our conscious attitudes and acts?

Properly conducted, this review will lead us to the usual source of our thoughtforms. If the source is negative and polluted, we must recognize the need to reform our assumptions and purify our thoughts and feelings. On the other hand, if the source is the best within us and our environment, then we will know that we have the Midas touch. We consistently enrich human life through our thoughts and feelings.

ENLIGHTENMENT

The Revelation of Light is a compilation of 14 lessons on the psychic aspects of human life from the Enlightenment series written by Robert R. Leichtman, M.D. and Carl Japikse and published by Ariel Press.

In addition to this topic, the *Enlightenment* series includes six other books, each deaing with a specific area of enlightenment:

- *The Light of Learning,* which explores the principles of personal and spiritual growth.
- *The Lights of Heaven,* an exploration of the archetypal forces of the mind of God.
- *Embodying the Light,* a guide to enlightened self-expression and how it can enrich our lives.
- *Embracing the Light,* in which the process and techniques of spiritual integration are described.
- *The Light Which Penetrates,* an examination of the use of the mind to nourish itself on the wonderful advances of human civilization.
- *Companions in the Light* examines other forms of life on earth and how a reverence for the beauty and glory of all life enriches our own.

Each of these books may be purchased for $15 apiece. The entire set of 7 books may be ordered for $90. Please enclose a shipping fee of $6 for one book and $8 for two or more books. Ask for a quote on shipping charges outside of the United States.

OTHER BOOKS FROM ARIEL PRESS

IN THE DAYS OF THE COMET
A novel by H.G. Wells, $15

THE ART OF LIVING
A five-volume set of essays
By Robert R. Leichtman, M.D. & Carl Japikse
$64

THE LIFE OF SPIRIT
A five-volume set of essays
By Robert R. Leichtman, M.D. & Carl Japikse
$64

FAITH FATIGUE
By Robert R. Leichtman, M.D., $18

THE STORY OF GOD
By Carl Japikse, $18

ACTIVE MEDITATION
By Robert R. Leichtman, M.D. & Carl Japikse
$32

PRACTICAL MYSTICISM
by Evelyn Underhill, $16

THE GIFT OF HEALING
by Ambrose & Olga Worrall, $18

ORDERING

Our books can be purchased online from amazon.com or through your favorite bookstore. They may also be ordered directly from Ariel Press. Please check out our website at http://lightariel.com. Orders may be entered through this website, or by telephoning Ariel Press at (770) 894-4226 any time Tuesday or Wednesday during normal office hours.

We accept PayPal, major credit cards, and checks. To order by check, please send your order to Light, 88 North Gate Station Drive #106, Marble Hill, GA 30148.

Please inquire if you wish to purchase any of our books in ebook format.